Math in Focus®

Singapore Math®
by Marshall Cavendish

Student Edition

Program Consultant and Author
Dr. Fong Ho Kheong

Authors
Gan Kee Soon
Dr. Ng Wee Leng

Course
1B

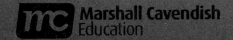

Marshall Cavendish
Education

U.S. Distributor

Houghton Mifflin Harcourt.
The Learning Company™

Contents

8 **Equations and Inequalities**

Chapter Opener

How can you use equations and inequalities to describe situations and solve real-world problems?

RECALL PRIOR KNOWLEDGE

Finding the missing number in an equation • Comparing numbers with symbols

• Using variables to write algebraic expressions • Evaluating algebraic expressions

• Plotting points on a coordinate plane

▶ Activity

Chapter

The Coordinate Plane

▶ Activity

10 Area of Polygons

Surface Area and Volume of Solids

© 2020 Marshall Cavendish Education Pte Ltd

x Contents

12 Introduction to Statistics

Chapter Opener 265

How can you represent numerical data and use them to answer statistical questions?

RECALL PRIOR KNOWLEDGE 266

Interpreting data in a line plot

▶ Activity

13 Measures of Central Tendency and Variability

▶ Activity

Manipulative List

Craft sticks

Geometric sets

Preface

Welcome!

Math in Focus® is a program that puts **you** at the center of an exciting learning experience! This experience is all about equipping you with critical thinking skills and mathematical strategies, explaining your thinking to deepen your understanding, and helping you to become a skilled and confident problem solver.

What's in your book?

Each chapter in this book begins with a real-world situation of the math topic you are about to learn.

In each chapter, you will encounter the following features:

THINK introduces a problem for the whole section, to stimulate creative and critical thinking and help you hone your problem-solving skills. You may not be able to answer the problem right away but you can revisit it a few times as you build your knowledge through the section.

ENGAGE consists of tasks that link what you already know with what you will be learning next. The tasks allow you to explore and discuss mathematical concepts with your classmates.

LEARN introduces new mathematical concepts through a Concrete-Pictorial-Abstract (C-P-A) approach, using activities and examples.

Activity comprises learning experiences that promote collaboration with your classmates. These activities allow you to reinforce your learning or uncover new mathematical concepts.

TRY supports and reinforces your learning through guided practice.

INDEPENDENT PRACTICE allows you to work on a variety of problems and apply the concepts and skills you have learned to solve these problems on your own.

Additional features include:

RECALL PRIOR KNOWLEDGE	 Math Talk	MATH SHARING	⚠ Caution, and Math Note
Helps you recall related concepts you learned before, accompanied by practice questions	Invites you to explain your reasoning and communicate your ideas to your classmates and teachers	Encourages you to create strategies, discover methods, and share them with your classmates and teachers using mathematical language	Highlights common errors and misconceptions, as well as provides you with useful hints and reminders
LET'S EXPLORE	**MATH JOURNAL**	**PUT ON YOUR THINKING CAP!**	**CHAPTER WRAP–UP**
Extends your learning through investigative activities	Allows you to reflect on your learning when you write down your thoughts about the mathematical concepts learned	Challenges you to apply the mathematical concepts to solve problems, and also hones your critical thinking skills	Summarizes your learning in a flow chart and helps you to make connections within the chapter
CHAPTER REVIEW	**Assessment Prep**	**PERFORMANCE TASK**	**STEAM**
Provides you with ample practice in the concepts learned	Prepares you for state tests with assessment-type problems	Assesses your learning through problems that allow you to demonstrate your understanding and knowledge	Promotes collaboration with your classmates through interesting projects that allow you to use math in creative ways

Are you ready to experience math the Singapore way? Let's go!

How much do you know about designing a backyard?

Algebraic expressions are found in practically all formulas. A landscape gardener can use formulas to find out the amount of materials required for a backyard or the cost of a project. Suppose the landscape gardener wants to build a rectangular flower bed. He has to calculate the amount of soil needed for the flower bed. He can use the formula Volume = length × width × height or simply $V = lwh$.

In this chapter, you will learn how to form algebraic expressions. The skill will allow you to solve problems simply.

?

How can you use algebraic expressions?

Name: _____ Date: _____

Using bar models to show the four operations

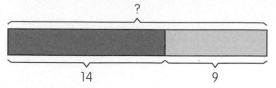

$? = 14 + 9$
$\quad = 23$

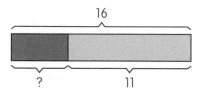

$? = 16 - 11$
$\quad = 5$

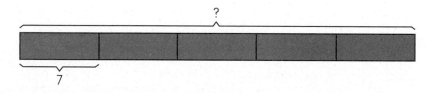

$? = 5 \cdot 7$
$\quad = 35$

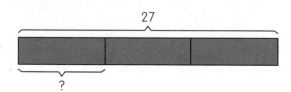

$? = 27 \div 3$
$\quad = 9$

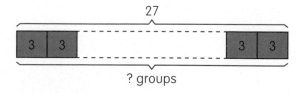

$? = 27 \div 3$
$\quad = 9$

© 2020 Marshall Cavendish Education Pte Ltd

▶ **Quick Check**

Draw a bar model to show each operation.

1 15 + 4

2 17 − 9

3 6 · 5

4 28 ÷ 4

Finding common factors and greatest common factor of two whole numbers

List the common factors of 6 and 14.
Then, find their greatest common factor.

6 = 1 · 6
6 = 2 · 3

14 = 1 · 14
14 = 2 · 7

Factors of 6: ①, ②, 3, and 6

Factors of 14: ①, ②, 7, and 14

The common factors of 6 and 14 are 1 and 2.
The greatest common factor of 6 and 14 is 2.

▶ **Quick Check**

Find the common factors and greatest common factor of each pair of numbers.

5 6 and 9

6 4 and 12

7 5 and 15

8 8 and 28

Meaning of mathematical terms

The sum of 3 and 4 is 3 + 4.

The difference "3 less than 4" is 4 − 3.

The product of 3 and 4 is 3 · 4.

The quotient "divide 3 by 4" is 3 ÷ 4 or $\frac{3}{4}$.

3 is the dividend and 4 is the divisor.

▶ **Quick Check**

Fill in each blank with **quotient, sum, difference, product, dividend,** or **divisor.**

9 The _____ "5 less than 7" is 7 − 5.

10 The _____ "divide 5 by 7" is $\frac{5}{7}$.

7 is the _____ and 5 is the _____.

11 The _____ of 5 and 7 is 7 · 5.

12 The _____ of 5 and 7 is 5 + 7.

Using Letters to Represent Numbers

Learning Objectives:
- Use a letter to represent an unknown number.
- Write simple algebraic expressions.

New Vocabulary
algebraic expression
variable
term (of an expression)

THINK

For every two pens that Bryan has, Jason has three pens. If Jason has x pens, how many pens does Bryan have?

ENGAGE

Lily buys some plants. Her friend gives her 2 more plants. How many plants does Lily have now? Explain your thinking. How do you express the number of plants Lily has now? Discuss.

LEARN Use letters to represent unknown numbers and write ~~algebraic expressions~~ by adding

1 Ana has 3 apples.

a If she gets 1 more apple, how many apples does she have now?

3 + 1 = 4

Ana has 4 apples now.

b If she gets 4 more apples, how many apples does she have now?

3 + 4 = 7

Ana has 7 apples now.

c If her friend gives her some apples, how many apples does she have now?

> Her friend gives her an unknown number of apples. You can use the letter x to represent the unknown number. The letter x can represent any number.

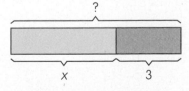

Ana has (x + 3) apples now.

Math Note

x is called a variable. A variable can take different values.
If Ana's friend gave her 6 apples, then $x = 6$.

x + 3 is an example of an algebraic expression in terms of x.
x and 3 are the terms of this expression.

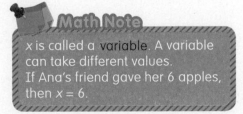

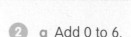
2 a Add 0 to 6.

   $6 + 0 = 6$

b Add 0 to x.

   $x + 0 = x$

3 a Sum of 11 and 3

   $11 + 3 = 14$

b Sum of n and 3

   $n + 3$

4 a 4 more than 8

   $8 + 4 = 12$

b 4 more than y

   $y + 4$

$6 + 0 = 0 + 6 = 6$
$x + 0 = 0 + x = x$

Math Talk

Is $x + 5$ the same as $5 + x$? Explain.

TRY Practice using letters to represent unknown numbers and writing algebraic expressions by adding

Fill in the table.

1 Mr. Garcia is a mathematics teacher. His students do not know his age. Let Mr. Garcia be x years old now. Find Mr. Garcia's age in terms of x.

Description	Mr. Garcia's Age (Years)
Mr. Garcia's age now	x
Mr. Garcia's age 3 years from now	
Mr. Garcia's age 5 years from now	
Mr. Garcia's age 10 years from now	

Write an algebraic expression for each statement.

2 Add 6 to y.

3 Sum of z and 8

4 3 more than p

5 q more than 10

ENGAGE

There are 35 students in Mr. Green's class. There are fewer students in Ms. Martin's class. How many more students are in Mr. Green's class than Ms. Martin's? Draw a model to show your thinking. Is there more than one way to represent this situation? Explain.

LEARN Write algebraic expressions by subtracting

1 Paige has 20 granola bars.

   a Kyle has 5 granola bars. How many more granola bars does Paige have than Kyle?

   $20 - 5 = 15$

   Paige has 15 more granola bars than Kyle.

   b Kyle has 12 granola bars. How many more granola bars does Paige have than Kyle?

   $20 - 12 = 8$

   Paige has 8 more granola bars than Kyle.

   c Kyle has y granola bars. How many more granola bars does Paige have than Kyle?

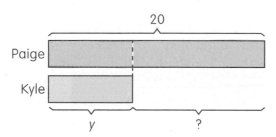

   Paige has $(20 - y)$ more granola bars than Kyle.

   $20 - y$ is an algebraic expression in terms of y.

   20 and y are the terms of this expression.

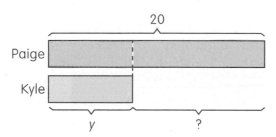

Math Talk

Nicole wants to know whether $20 - y$ is the same as $y - 20$. How can you explain to her?

2 a Subtract 3 from 7.

   $7 - 3 = 4$

   b Subtract 3 from a.

   $a - 3$

3 a 1 less than 12

   $12 - 1 = 11$

   b 1 less than x

   $x - 1$

3 **a** Divide 18 by 9.

$18 \div 9 = 2$

b Divide n by 9.

$n \div 9 = \frac{n}{9}$

> The quotient of n divided by 9 is $\frac{n}{9}$. n is the dividend and 9 is the divisor.

4 Divide the product of 7 and n by 5.

$7 \cdot n \div 5 = \frac{7n}{5}$

Activity Drawing models to represent algebraic expressions

Work in pairs.

① Describe the algebraic expression $3w$ in as many ways as you can.

② Draw a bar model for the algebraic expression in ①. Compare your answers in ① and ②.

③ Repeat ① and ② with each of the following algebraic expressions.

a $5z$

b $\frac{g}{4}$

c $\frac{120 - n}{3}$

d $\frac{k + 25}{2}$

TRY Practice writing algebraic expressions by dividing

Fill in the table.

① There were m cards in a pack. They were shared equally among some children. Find the number of cards each child received in terms of m.

Number of Children	1	4	6	8	12
Number of Cards Each Child Received	m				

Write an algebraic expression for each statement.

② Divide n by 7.

③ Divide the sum of r and 11 by 4.

INDEPENDENT PRACTICE

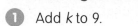

Write an algebraic expression for each statement.

1 Add k to 9.

2 Sum of 4 and p

3 r more than 7

4 Subtract 5 from n.

5 Subtract q from 6.

6 x less than 8

7 x groups of 3

8 Multiply 7 by m.

9 Product of 12 and r

10 Divide s by 5.

11 Bianca is now x years old.

  a Her father is 24 years older than her. Find her father's age in terms of x.

  b Her brother is 2 years younger than her. Find her brother's age in terms of x.

  c Her sister is twice as old as her. Find her sister's age in terms of x.

  d Her cousin is $\frac{1}{3}$ of her age. Find her cousin's age in terms of x.

12 Add $\frac{1}{5}$ to the product of 4 and c.

13 Divide the sum of 8 and e by 9.

14 Multiply *k* by 5. Then, add 3 to the product.

15 Divide *m* by 7. Then, subtract 4 from the quotient.

16 A number that is 7 more than 3 times *x*

17 The total cost, in cents, of 8 apples and 9 oranges if each apple costs 2*y* cents and each orange costs 80 cents

18 The perimeter of a triangle whose sides are 4*z* units, 10 units, and 15 units

Solve.

19 Ms. Wilson bought 5 pencils for *w* dollars. Each pen cost 35 cents more than a pencil. Write an algebraic expression for each statement in terms of *w*.

   a The cost, in dollars, of a pen

   b The number of pencils that Ms. Wilson can buy with 20 dollars

20 The figure shown is formed by a rectangle and a square.

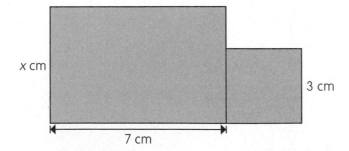

Express the area of the figure in terms of *x*.

2 Evaluating Algebraic Expressions

Learning Objective:
• Evaluate algebraic expressions for given values of the variables.

New Vocabulary
evaluate
substitute

💡THINK

Mr. Walker has y $2 bills. He spends $3 and saves half of what is left. Write an expression, in terms of y, for the amount he saves and evaluate the expression when $y = 12$.

ENGAGE

1. Draw a bar model to represent each of the following:

   a $8 + 4$ **b** $8 - 4$ **c** 8×4 **d** $8 \div 4$

   How are the models different? How are they the same? Discuss.

2. Replace one of the terms in each expression with a variable. Then, write a simple story for each expression.

LEARN algebraic expressions for given values of the variables

1. Evaluate $x + 5$ when $x = 9$.

   When $x = 9$,
   $$x + 5 = \mathbf{9} + 5$$
   $$= 14$$

> To evaluate an algebraic expression for a given value of the variable, substitute the given value of the variable into the expression. Then, find the value of the expression.

2. Evaluate $30 - y$ when $y = 6$.

   When $y = 6$,
   $$30 - \mathbf{y} = 30 - \mathbf{6}$$
   $$= 24$$

3. Evaluate $8p$ when $p = 7$.

   When $p = 7$,
   $$8\mathbf{p} = 8 \cdot \mathbf{p}$$
   $$= 8 \cdot 7$$
   $$= 56$$

4. Evaluate $\frac{q}{10}$ when $q = 60$.

   When $q = 60$,
   $$\frac{\mathbf{q}}{10} = \frac{\mathbf{60}}{10}$$
   $$= 6$$

5. Evaluate $\frac{m}{4} - 9$ when $m = 36$.

   When $m = 36$,
   $$\frac{\mathbf{m}}{4} - 9 = \frac{\mathbf{36}}{4} - 9$$
   $$= 9 - 9$$
   $$= 0$$

TRY Practice evaluating algebraic expressions for given values of the variables

Evaluate each algebraic expression for the given values of z.

①

Expression	Value of Expression When $z = 8$	Value of Expression When $z = 16$
$12 + z$		
$25 - z$		
$3z - 14$		
$\frac{z}{16} + 15$		

Evaluate each algebraic expression when $q = 20$.

② $\dfrac{4 + 2q}{11}$

③ $\dfrac{125 + q}{7}$

④ $\dfrac{11q}{4} + 25$

Solve.

⑤ There are n apples in each box. Write an expression in terms of n for each statement and evaluate the expression when $n = 24$.

   a The number of apples left in a box after 6 apples have been eaten

   b The number of apples each child gets when a whole box of apples is shared equally among 4 children

   c The number of apples each child gets when a whole box of apples and another 11 apples are shared equally among 5 children

⑥ Kaitlyn is x years old now. Write an expression in terms of x for each statement and evaluate the expression when $x = 18$.

   a Kaitlyn's brother is 5 years older than her. Find his age.

   b Kaitlyn's aunt is twice as old as her. Find her aunt's age.

   c Kaitlyn's cousin is half her age. Find her cousin's age.

Name: _____   Date: _____

Evaluate each expression for the given value of the variable.

1. $3x + 5$ when $x = 5$

2. $5y - 8$ when $y = 3$

3. $40 - 9y$ when $y = 2$

4. $\frac{7w}{6}$ when $w = 18$

5. $4 + \frac{5z}{6}$ when $z = 12$

6. $\frac{4 + 5z}{6}$ when $z = 12$

7. $\frac{8r}{9} - 15$ when $r = 27$

8. $16 - \frac{2u - 4}{3}$ when $u = 18$

Solve.

9. There are x granola bars in each box. Write an expression in terms of x for each statement and evaluate the expression when $x = 35$.

    a The number of granola bars in 5 boxes

    b The number of granola bars each child gets when a box of granola bars and 5 granola bars are shared equally among 10 children

10 Hana is y years old. Write an expression in terms of y for each statement and evaluate the expression when $y = 14$.

    a Hana's brother is 10 years younger than twice her age. Find his age.

    b Hana's neighbor is 5 years older than half her age. Find her neighbor's age.

Evaluate each expression when $x = 3$.

11 $\dfrac{x+1}{2} + \dfrac{5x-3}{10}$

12 $\dfrac{11+x}{2} - \dfrac{9x-3}{4}$

13 $\dfrac{7x-6}{3} + 4(8+2x)$

14 $13(11-3x) - \dfrac{5(16-4x)}{2}$

Evaluate each statement when $y = 7$.

15 Sum of $\dfrac{y}{3}$ and $\dfrac{4y}{9}$

16 Product of $(y+1)$ and $(y-1)$

17 Subtract $\dfrac{14y+37}{5}$ from $8(2y-1)$

18 Divide $9(7y-15)$ by $\dfrac{110-6y}{4}$

3 Simplifying Algebraic Expressions

Learning Objectives:
• Simplify algebraic expressions in one variable.
• Recognize that the simplified and original expressions are equivalent.

New Vocabulary
coefficient
equivalent expressions
like terms
unlike terms

 THINK

Steven simplifies $a + 2a + 3$ to get $6a$. Explain why you agree or disagree with him.

ENGAGE

1. Use cubes to show 2 groups of 3. How many cubes are there?

2. Maria bought 2 equal bags of apples. Draw a bar model to represent the situation. How would you express the total number of apples in the bags? Explain.

LEARN Simplify algebraic expressions involving addition

1. A rod of length a meters is joined to another rod that is also a meters long. What is the total length of the two rods?

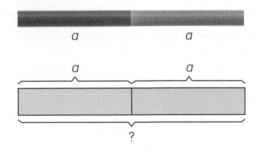

Total length of the two rods = $(a + a)$ m

$$a + a = 2 \cdot a$$
$$= 2a$$

You can simplify $(a + a)$ as $2a$.

The total length of the two rods is $2a$ meters.

In the term $2a$, 2 is called the coefficient of a.

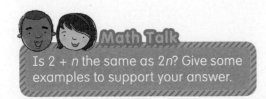

Math Talk

Is $2 + n$ the same as $2n$? Give some examples to support your answer.

2 Alan, Bruno, and Pedro have b dollars each. Find the total amount of money they have.

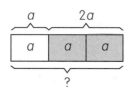

Total amount of money = $\$(b + b + b)$
$$b + b + b = 3 \cdot b$$
$$= 3b$$

The total amount of money they have is $3b$ dollars.

In the term $3b$, 3 is called the coefficient of b.

3 Simplify $a + 2a$.

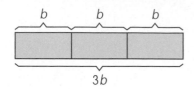

$$a + 2a = 3a$$

$a + 2a$ and $3a$ are equivalent expressions because they are equal for all values of a.

a and $2a$ are the terms of the expression $a + 2a$.
a and $2a$ are called like terms.

4 Simplify $2a + 3a$.

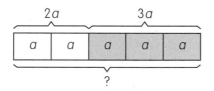

$$2a + 3a = a + a + a + a + a$$
$$= 5a$$

$$2a + 3a = 5a$$

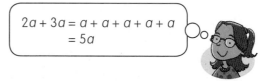

Math Talk
Is $2a + 3a$ the same as $3a + 2a$? Explain.

TRY Practice simplifying algebraic expressions involving addition

Simplify each expression.

1 $b + b + b + b + b + b$

2 $x + 3x$

3 $3y + 6y$

4 $4c + 2c + 5c$

ENGAGE

Mr. Thomas bought 5 equal boxes of erasers.
He gave away 2 of the boxes.
Draw a bar model to show the number of erasers left.
Share your model with your partner.

LEARN Simplify algebraic expressions involving subtraction

1. Simplify $3a - a$.

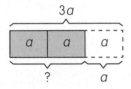

$3a - a = 2a$

2. Simplify $5a - 2a$.

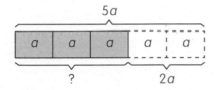

$5a - 2a = 3a$

3. Simplify $4a - 3a - a$.

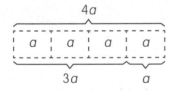

Math Note

Any term that is subtracted from itself is equal to 0.

$4a - 3a - a = a - a$
$\qquad\qquad\quad = 0$

TRY Practice simplifying algebraic expressions involving subtraction

Simplify each expression.

1. $5p - p$

2. $10x - 6x$

3. $8y - 3y - 5y$

4. $12z - 6z - z$

ENGAGE

Riley collected some comic books. Justin collected twice as many comic books as Riley. They then gave away 10 comic books to their friends. Draw a bar model to show the total number of comic books they have left.

LEARN Simplify algebraic expressions using order of operations

Activity Writing and simplifying algebraic expressions

Work in pairs.

Let the length of each craft stick equal *p* units.

1. Form a closed figure using 3 or more craft sticks.

   Example:

2. Write the total length of the craft sticks used.

3. Remove 1 or more craft sticks, and then add craft sticks to form another figure.

   Example:

    remove 1 craft stick, add 3 craft sticks →

4. Write the total length of the craft sticks used in the new figure. Subtract the total length of the craft sticks removed and add the total length of the craft sticks added.

5. Check your answer in ④ by counting the number of craft sticks used in the new figure to find the total length.

6. Repeat the activity with other figures.

1 Simplify $6a + 3a - 2a$.

$$6a + 3a - 2a = 9a - 2a$$
$$= 7a$$

Work from left to right. Add. Subtract.

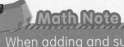

Math Note

When adding and subtracting algebraic terms with no brackets, always work from left to right. For example, $6a - 2a + 3a = 4a + 3a$ and $6a - 2a + 3a \neq 6a - 5a$.

2 Simplify $6a - 2a + 3a$.

$$6a - 2a + 3a = 4a + 3a$$
$$= 7a$$

Work from left to right. Subtract. Add.

3 Find the distance from Point A to Point B.

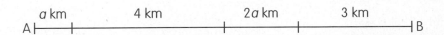

| a km | 4 km | 2a km | 3 km |

A ├───┼─────────┼─────────┼─────────┤ B

Total distance $= a + 4 + 2a + 3$
$$= a + 2a + 4 + 3$$
$$= (3a + 7) \text{ km}$$

The distance from Point A to Point B is $(3a + 7)$ kilometers.

Math Note

Commutative Property of Addition: Two numbers can be added in any order. So, $4 + 2a = 2a + 4$.

In this expression, a and $2a$ are like terms. So are 4 and 3. Only like terms can be simplified. $3a + 7$ cannot be simplified further. $3a$ and 7 are unlike terms.

4 Simplify $4x + 6 - 3x$.

$$4x + 6 - \mathbf{3x} = 4x - \mathbf{3x} + 6$$
$$= x + 6$$

Math Talk

Is $3 + x$ the same as $3x$? Explain.

TRY Practice simplifying algebraic expressions using order of operations

Simplify each expression.

1 $2x + 3x - 4x$

2 $x + 5x - 6x$

3 $b + 6 + b + 5$

4 $3b + 4b + 2 + 6$

5 $5s + 9 - 3s$

6 $8s + 6 - 2s - 1$

Name: _____   Date: _____

INDEPENDENT PRACTICE

Simplify each expression. Then, state the coefficient of the variable in each expression.

1 $u + u + u + u$

2 $v + v + 5 - 2$

3 $w + w + w + w + w + w + 15 - 7$

Simplify each expression.

4 $3p + p$

5 $7p - 2p$

6 $3p - 2p + 5p$

7 $2p + 3p + 4p + 5p - 6p - 7p$

8 $36a + 12 - 6a - 7$

9 $21 + 34b - 8 - 5b + 8 + 23b$

State whether each pair of expressions is equivalent.

10 $5x$ and $x + x + 3x$

11 $4y + 2y + y$ and $5y + y$

12 $2z + 5$ and $z + 8 + z - 3$

13 $2w - 5$ and $5 - 2w$

14 $11u - 4u$ and $11 - 4 + u$

15 $3v + v$ and $\frac{12v}{3}$

Solve.

16 At present, Laila is *h* years old, Henry is 2*h* years old, and Ivan is 8 years old. Find an expression for each person's age in *h* years' time. Then, find an expression for the sum of their ages in *h* years' time.

17 The adults and children in a neighborhood attended a party. There were 18 children. There were *w* fewer children than adults. How many people were there at the party?

18 A rectangular backyard has a length of (*y* + 2) yards and a width of (4*y* – 1) yards. Find the perimeter of the backyard in terms of *y*.

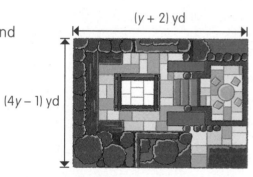

19 Ms. Nelson had 64*b* dollars. She gave $\frac{1}{8}$ of it to her son and spent $45.

How much money did Ms. Nelson have left? Express your answer in terms of *b*.

20 A rectangle has a length of (2*m* + 1) units and a width of (10 – *m*) units.

A square has sides of length $\frac{2m + 1}{2}$ units.

a Find the perimeter of the rectangle.

b Find the perimeter of the square.

c Find the sum of the perimeters of the two figures if *m* = 6.

d If *m* = 6, the perimeter of the rectangle is greater than the perimeter of the square. How many units greater is the perimeter of the rectangle than the perimeter of the square?

4 Expanding and Factoring Algebraic Expressions

Learning Objectives:
- Expand simple algebraic expressions.
- Factor simple algebraic expressions.

New Vocabulary
expand

THINK

Gianna thinks that $4n + 32$ and $4(n + 8)$ are equivalent expressions. Use bar models to explain whether she is right or wrong.

ENGAGE

Mason has 2 boxes. Each box contains 4 pens and the same number of pencils. What is the possible number of pens in the 2 boxes? If there are fewer than 7 pencils in each box, what are the possible numbers of pencils in the 2 boxes? Explain to your partner how you get the answer.

LEARN Use the distributive property to  algebraic expressions

1 Expand $2(r + 8)$.

$2(r + 8)$ means 2 groups of $r + 8$:

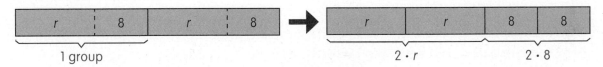

r	8	r	8

1 group   →   2 · r   2 · 8

Rearrange the terms to collect the like terms:

| r | r | 8 | 8 |

From the models,

$$2(r + 8) = 2 \cdot (r + 8)$$
$$= 2 \cdot r + 2 \cdot 8$$
$$= 2r + 16$$

$2 \cdot (r + 8)$
$= (r + 8) + (r + 8)$
$= r + r + 8 + 8$
$= 2r + 16$

$2(r + 8)$ and $2r + 16$ are equivalent expressions because they are equal for all values of r.
If $r = 2$, $2(r + 8) = 20$ and $2r + 16 = 20$.
If $r = 6$, $2(r + 8) = 28$ and $2r + 16 = 28$.

$2r + 16$ is the expanded form of $2(r + 8)$.

2 Expand $3(k + 6)$.

$3(k + 6)$ means 3 groups of $k + 6$:

| k | 6 | k | 6 | k | 6 |

1 group

Rearrange the terms to collect the like terms:

| k | k | k | 6 | 6 | 6 |

$3 \cdot k$ $3 \cdot 6$

From the models,

$$\mathbf{3}(k + 6) = \mathbf{3} \cdot (k + 6)$$
$$= \mathbf{3} \cdot k + \mathbf{3} \cdot 6$$
$$= 3k + 18$$

$3 \cdot (k + 6)$
$= (k + 6) + (k + 6) + (k + 6)$
$= k + k + k + 6 + 6 + 6$
$= 3k + 18$

$3(k + 6)$ and $3k + 18$ are equivalent expressions because they are equal for all values of k.

$3k + 18$ is the expanded form of $3(k + 6)$.

Activity **Recognizing that expanded expressions are equivalent** ────

Work in pairs.

1 Draw a rectangle with a width of 2 centimeters and a length longer than 3 centimeters on a piece of paper.

$(p + 3)$ cm

2 cm

2 Find the area of the rectangle in terms of p.

© 2020 Marshall Cavendish Education Pte Ltd

③ Divide the rectangle into two rectangles, A and B, as shown.

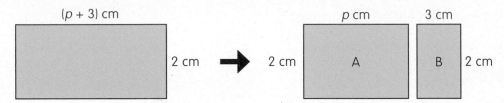

④ Find the areas of Rectangles A and B.

⑤ Using your answers found in ② and ④, state how the three areas are related.

⑥ Repeat the activity using rectangles of different sizes.

TRY Practice using the distributive property to expand algebraic expressions

Expand each expression.

① $3(x + 4)$

② $6(2x + 3)$

③ $2(7 + 6x)$

④ $5(y - 3)$

⑤ $4(4y - 1)$

⑥ $9(5x - 2)$

State whether each pair of expressions is equivalent.

⑦ $6(x + 5)$ and $6x + 30$

⑧ $7(x + 3)$ and $21 + 7x$

⑨ $4(y - 4)$ and $4y - 4$

⑩ $3(y - 6)$ and $18 - 3y$

ENGAGE

Shanti has 4 red sticks and 2 blue sticks as shown.

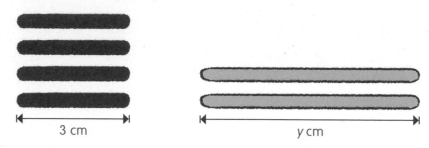

3 cm

y cm

Write different possible expressions to show the total length of the 6 sticks.
Explain to your partner how you get the answers.

LEARN Factor algebraic expressions by taking out a common factor

1. You can expand the expression $3(4z + 1)$ by writing it as $12z + 3$.
   You can also start with the expression $12z + 3$ and write it as $3(4z + 1)$.
   When you write $12z + 3$ as $3(4z + 1)$, you have factored $12z + 3$.

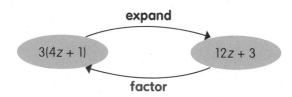

expand

$3(4z + 1)$ $12z + 3$

factor

2. Factor $2y + 10$.

   $$\begin{aligned} 2y + 10 &= \mathbf{2} \cdot y + \mathbf{2} \cdot 5 \\ &= \mathbf{2} \cdot (y + 5) \qquad \text{Take out the common factor, 2.} \\ &= 2(y + 5) \end{aligned}$$

   $2(y + 5)$ is the factored form of $2y + 10$.

   > $10 = 1 \cdot 10 \qquad 2y = 1 \cdot 2y$
   > $10 = 2 \cdot 5 \qquad 2y = 2 \cdot y$
   > Excluding 1, the common factor of 10 and $2y$ is 2.

   ### Check

   Expand the expression $2(y + 5)$ to check the factoring.

   $$\begin{aligned} 2(y + 5) &= 2 \cdot y + 2 \cdot 5 \\ &= 2y + 10 \end{aligned}$$

   $2y + 10$ is factored correctly.

   > Factoring is the inverse of expanding. You can use expanding to check if you have factored an expression correctly.

   > Since $2y + 10$ and $2(y + 5)$ are equal for all values of y, they are equivalent expressions.

3 Factor $6z - 9$.

$9 = 1 \cdot 9$ $6z = 1 \cdot 6z$
$9 = 3 \cdot 3$ $6z = 2 \cdot 3z$
               $6z = 3 \cdot 2z$
               $6z = 6 \cdot z$
Excluding 1, the common factor of 9 and $6z$ is 3.

$6z - 9 = \mathbf{3} \cdot 2z - \mathbf{3} \cdot 3$
$ = \mathbf{3} \cdot (2z - 3)$ Take out the common factor, 3.
$ = 3(2z - 3)$

$3(2z - 3)$ is the factored form of $6z - 9$.

4 Factor $12 - 4k$.

$12 = 1 \cdot 12$ $4k = 1 \cdot 4k$
$12 = 2 \cdot 6$ $4k = 2 \cdot 2k$
$12 = 3 \cdot 4$ $4k = 4 \cdot k$
Excluding 1, the common factor of 12 and $4k$ are 2 and 4. Hence the greatest common factor is 4.

$12 - 4k = \mathbf{4} \cdot 3 - \mathbf{4} \cdot k$
$ = \mathbf{4} \cdot (3 - k)$ Take out the greatest common factor, 4.
$ = 4(3 - k)$

$4(3 - k)$ is the factored form of $12 - 4k$.

When you write $12 - 4k$ as $4(3 - k)$, it is completely factored because the terms 3 and k have no more common factors.

TRY Practice factoring algebraic expressions by taking out a common factor

Factor each expression.

1. $3x + 3$

2. $4x + 6$

3. $8 + 6y$

4. $5y - 10$

5. $4 - 10z$

6. $12 - 8x$

7. $8f + 6$

8. $12t - 8$

9. $15 + 5q$

10. $32m - 40$

State whether each pair of expressions is equivalent.

11. $8x + 6$ and $2(4x + 3)$

12. $3(y + 6)$ and $18 + 3y$

13. $5x - 10$ and $5(x - 5)$

14. $4(y - 4)$ and $16 - 4y$

15. $3(x + 5)$ and $15 + 3x$

16. $12 - 8y$ and $4(2y - 3)$

INDEPENDENT PRACTICE

Expand each expression.

1 $5(x + 2)$

2 $7(2x - 3)$

3 $3(x + 11)$

4 $9(4x - 7)$

Factor each expression.

5 $6p + 6$

6 $12 + 3q$

7 $14r - 8$

8 $12r - 12$

State whether each pair of expressions is equivalent.

9 $4x + 12$ and $4(x + 3)$

10 $5(x - 1)$ and $5x - 1$

11 $7(5 + y)$ and $7y + 35$

12 $9(y - 2)$ and $18 - 9y$

Expand and simplify each expression.

13 $3(m + 2) + 4(6 + m)$

14 $5(2p + 5) + 4(2p - 3)$

15 $4(6k + 7) + 9 - 14k$

Simplify each expression. Then, factor the expression.

16 $14x + 13 - 8x - 1$

17 $8(y + 3) + 6 - 3y$

18 $4(3z + 7) + 5(8 + 6z)$

Solve.

19 Expand and simplify the expression $3(x - 2) + 9(x + 1) + 5(1 + 2x) + 2(3x - 4)$.

20 Are the two expressions equivalent? Justify your reasoning.

$15(y + 6) + 10(y - 5) + 20(2y + 3)$ and $5(20 + 13y)$

21 A yard of lace costs w cents and a yard of fabric costs 40 cents more than the yard of lace. Melanie wants to buy 1 yard of lace and 2 yards of fabric. How much money will she need? Express your answer in terms of w.

22 The average weight of 6 packages is $(9m + 8)$ pounds. 2 more packages, with weights of $(12m + 12)$ pounds and $(14m + 12)$ pounds, are added to the original 6 packages. Find the average weight of the 8 packages.

23 The figure shows two rectangles joined together to form Rectangle *ABCD*.

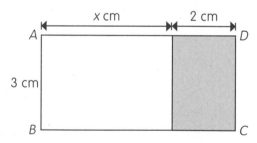

a Write the length of $\overline{BC}$ in terms of x. Then, write an expression for the area of Rectangle *ABCD* in terms of x.

b Find the area of each of the two smaller rectangles.

c **Mathematical Habit 2 Use mathematical reasoning**
Explain how you can use your answers in **a** and **b** to show that the following expressions are equivalent.

$$3x + 6 \text{ and } 3(x + 2)$$

5 Real-World Problems: Algebraic Expressions

Learning Objective:
• Solve real-world problems involving algebraic expressions.

THINK

Briella is *k* years old now. She will be half of her aunt's age in 5 years' time. Find her aunt's present age in terms of *k*. If Briella is 13 years old now, what is her aunt's present age?

ENGAGE

Zachary has *x* pens. Sofia has twice as many pens as Zachary. Sofia gives her sister 1 pe[n]. Draw a bar model to find the number of pens Sofia has more than Zachary. Compare you[r] bar model to your partner's.

LEARN Solve real-world problems involving algebraic expressions

1 Emma has *y* books. Matthew has 3 times as many books as Emma. Matthew buys anoth[er] 7 books.

a How many more books does Matthew have than Emma?
  Give your answer in terms of *y* in the simplest form.

b If Emma has 25 books, how many more books does
  Matthew have than Emma?

 Understand the problem.

> How many books does Emma have?
> How many times as many books does Matthew have compared to Emma?
> Who has more books? Emma or Matthew?
> How many books does Matthew buy?
> What do I need to find?

STEP 2 Think of a plan.
I can draw a model.

STEP 3 Carry out the plan.

a

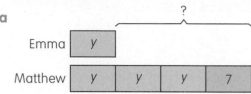

Matthew has $(3y + 7)$ books.

$3y + 7 - y = 2y + 7$

Matthew has $(2y + 7)$ more books than Emma.

b When $y = 25$,

$$2\mathbf{y} + 7 = (2 \times \mathbf{25}) + 7$$
$$= 50 + 7$$
$$= 57$$

Matthew has 57 more books than Emma.

STEP 4 Check the answers.
I can work backwards to check my answers.

a $y + 2y + 7 = 3y + 7$
  $3y + 7 - 7 = 3y$
  $3y \div 3 = y$
  Emma has y books.

b $25 + 57 = 82$
  $82 - 7 = 75$
  $75 \div 3 = 25$
  Emma has 25 books.

My answers are correct.

2. Ms. Davis had x dollars. She bought a dress for 35 dollars and spent the rest of her money on 3 identical notebooks.

a Find the price of 1 notebook in terms of x.

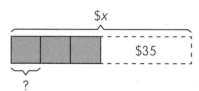

Price of 3 notebooks = $\$(x - 35)$

$$\$(x - 35) \div 3 = \$\left(\frac{x - 35}{3}\right)$$

The price of 1 notebook was $\left(\frac{x - 35}{3}\right)$ dollars.

b If Ms. Davis had 50 dollars, what was the price of 1 notebook?

When $x = 50$,

$$\frac{\mathbf{x} - 35}{3} = \frac{\mathbf{50} - 35}{3}$$
$$= \frac{15}{3}$$
$$= 5$$

The price of 1 notebook was 5 dollars.

Solve.

1   Some adults and children are watching a musical. There are *n* children.
There are 25 fewer adults than children.

   a Find the number of adults in terms of *n*.

   b If there are 124 children, how many adults are there?

2   Owen has *m* dollars and Lucas has $25 more.

   a Find the total amount of money they have in terms of *m*.

How much does Lucas
have in terms of *m*?

   b If *m* = 35, how much money do they have in all?

3 Mr. Peterson had *y* dollars in his wallet at first. After he withdrew $300 from the bank, he gave his wife half of the total amount of money he had.

a Find the amount of money he had left in terms of *y*.

b If Mr. Peterson had $60 in his wallet at first, how much money did he have left?

4 Ribbon A is *k* meters long. Ribbon B is twice as long as Ribbon A. Ribbon C is 1 meter shorter than Ribbon B.

a Find the length of Ribbon C in terms of *k*.

b If *k* = 3, how long is Ribbon C?

INDEPENDENT PRACTICE

Solve.

1 Natalia is *x* years old. Sarah is 3 times as old as her. Natalia is 5 years older than Alma.

   a Find Alma's age in terms of *x*.

   b Find Sarah's age in terms of *x*.

   c If *x* = 12, how much older is Sarah than Natalia?

2 A van travels from Town A to Town B. It uses 1 gallon of gas for every 24 miles traveled.

   a How many gallons of gas does the van use if it travels 3*x* miles?

   b The van uses 2*y* gallons of gas for its journey from Town A to Town B. Find the distance between Town A and Town B.

3 Luke bought *x* apples and some oranges. Luke bought 3 more oranges than apples. Each apple cost 40 cents and each orange cost 50 cents.

   a Find the number of pieces of fruit Luke bought in terms of *x*.

   b Find the total amount of money, in cents, that Luke spent on fruit. Give your answer in terms of *x*.

   c If Luke could have bought exactly 12 pears with the amount of money that was spent on the apples and oranges, find the cost of each pear, in cents, in terms of *x*.

24 A square backyard has a side length that is 3 meters shorter than the length of a rectangular backyard. Find the perimeter of the rectangular backyard in terms of y.

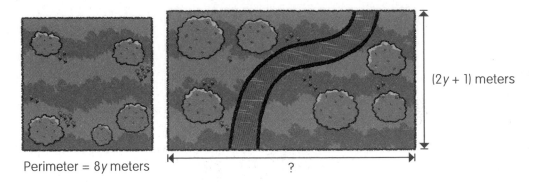

Perimeter = $8y$ meters

$(2y + 1)$ meters

?

25 Ms. Brooks sewed m shirts using 2 yards of cloth for each shirt. She also sewed $(m + 2)$ dresses using 5 yards of cloth for each dress.

a How much cloth did she use in all? Give your answer in terms of m.

b If $m = 7$, how much more cloth did she use to sew the dresses than the shirts?

26 A glass jug can hold $(p + 6)$ quarts less water than a plastic container. 2 glass jugs and 2 plastic containers contain $6p$ quarts of water in all.

    a How much water can the plastic container hold? Give your answer in terms of p.

    b If $p = 3$, find the amount of water, in quarts, 1 glass jug and 1 plastic container can hold in all.

27 Mr. Carter can paint 20 chairs in t hours. He uses 3 liters of paint for every 12 chairs that he painted.

    a Find, in terms of t, the number of chairs that he can paint in 3 hours.

    b Find, in terms of t, the time taken by Mr. Carter to paint 7 chairs.

    c If $t = 4$, find the amount of paint Mr. Carter has used after painting for 4 hours.

Assessment Prep

Answer each question.

28 Which expression represents "9 less than x"?

Ⓐ $x - 9$

Ⓑ $9 \cdot x$

Ⓒ $x + 9$

Ⓓ $9 - x$

29 Maya bought 12 pens for p dollars. Which expression can be used to determine the cost, in dollars, of 4 pens?

Ⓐ $3p$

Ⓑ $\frac{p}{3}$

Ⓒ $\frac{p}{4}$

Ⓓ $\frac{p}{12}$

30 Which expression is equivalent to $4(k - 5)$? Choose **all** that apply.

Ⓐ $4k - 5$

Ⓑ $4k - 20$

Ⓒ $5k - k - 5$

Ⓓ $k + 3k - 20$

Ⓔ $2(k - 5) + 2k$

31 What is the value of $3a + b^2 \div 2c - d$, when $a = 3$, $b = 4$, $c = 5$, and $d = 6$? Write your answer in the space below.

Name: _____ Date: _____

Design of a Community Garden

A group of students want to design and create a community garden. They do not know the exact measurements but they propose using a variable to represent the length and width of the garden. The length of the garden is 10 feet longer than the width.

1 Use a single variable to write algebraic expressions for both the length and width of the garden. Draw a diagram of the garden, labeling the length and width.

2 The students want to put a fence around the garden. Write an algebraic expression for the perimeter of the garden and then simplify it.

3 Write an algebraic expression for the area of the garden. Use mathematical terms to describe this expression.

4 If the width of the garden is 35 feet, how much fencing will be needed?

5 Halfway down the length of the garden, the students intend to plant a row of tomatoes. Write an algebraic expression for half of the length of the garden and then simplify it.

Rubric

Point(s)	Level	My Performance
7–8	4	• Most of my answers are correct. • I showed complete understanding of the concepts. • I used effective and efficient strategies to solve the problems. • I explained my answers and mathematical thinking clearly and completely.
5–6.5	3	• Some of my answers are correct. • I showed adequate understanding of the concepts. • I used effective strategies to solve the problems. • I explained my answers and mathematical thinking clearly.
3–4.5	2	• A few of my answers are correct. • I showed some understanding of the concepts. • I used some effective strategies to solve the problems. • I explained some of my answers and mathematical thinking clearly.
0–2.5	1	• A few of my answers are correct. • I showed little understanding of the concepts. • I used limited effective strategies to solve the problems. • I did not explain my answers and mathematical thinking clearly.

Teacher's Comments

STEAM

Paper Airplane Aerodynamics

For an aerodynamic object such as paper airplanes, four forces act on it:

- Thrust — the force that pushes the object forward through the air
- Drag — the force that resists the object's forward motion
- Gravity — the force that pushes the object downwards
- Lift — the force that pushes the object upwards

The shape of the object's wings affects lift. So, the four forces are important to the object's flight.

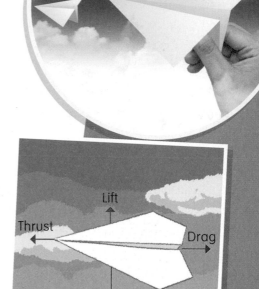

Task

Work in small groups to engineer a paper airplane.

1 Go to the library or go online to National Aeronautics and Space Administration (NASA)'s website to learn more about aerodynamics. View a variety of online videos to gather tips on making aerodynamic paper airplanes.

2 Design and make a paper airplane. Conduct several flight trials and measure or calculate the airplane's distance, speed, and time, where speed $= \frac{\text{distance}}{\text{time}}$, or $s = \frac{d}{t}$. Record the data in a table.

3 Modify the airplane's wings to improve one of the variables. Draw diagrams and take notes to show the changes you make. Conduct several trials. Collect data and record the results.

4 Share your results with other groups. Discuss the relationship between wing design and distance, speed, or time in the air.

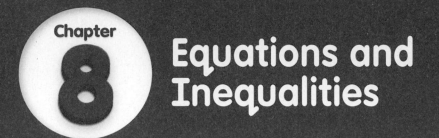
Equations and Inequalities

Going on a vacation?

If you travel to another country, you can use linear equations and inequalities to help you plan your finances. Before you leave, you might want to change your U.S. dollars into a different currency. The amount of money you get in the new currency depends on how many U.S. dollars you start with. It also depends on the currency exchange rate. To find the amount of money you get in the new currency, you can use a linear equation.

While on your trip, you may want to set aside money to spend on souvenirs. You can use a linear inequality to find how many souvenirs you can buy. Planning can be made easier by using linear equations and inequalities.

? How can you use equations and inequalities to describe situations and solve real-world problems?

Name: _____   Date: _____

Finding the missing number in an equation

Find each missing number.

a $\boxed{?} + 7 = 13$

$\boxed{?} = 6$

b $18 - \boxed{?} = 6$

$\boxed{?} = 12$

c $4 \cdot \boxed{?} = 24$

$\boxed{?} = 6$

$4 \times 6 = 24$
$24 \div 4 = 6$

d $\boxed{?} \div 7 = 8$

$\boxed{?} = 56$

$56 \div 7 = 8$
$8 \cdot 7 = 56$

▶ Quick Check

Find each missing number.

1 $14 + \underline{} = 19$

2 $\underline{} - 8 = 9$

3 $\underline{} \cdot 7 = 21$

4 $54 \div \underline{} = 6$

Comparing numbers with symbols

Symbol	Meaning	Example
=	is equal to	$12 \times 4 = 48$ → 12×4 is equal to 48.
≠	is not equal to	$6 - 2 \neq 2 - 6$ → $6 - 2$ is not equal to $2 - 6$.
>	is greater than	$0 > -9$ → 0 is greater than -9.
<	is less than	$-5 < -1$ → -5 is less than -1.

▶ Quick Check

Compare each pair of numbers or expressions using =, >, or <.

5 $25 \bigcirc -26$

6 $12 + 12 + 12 \bigcirc 3 \cdot 12$

7 $40 \div 8 \bigcirc 8 \div 40$

8 $-16 \bigcirc -7$

Using variables to write algebraic expressions

Statement	Expression
Sum of x and 7	$x + 7$
Subtract 14 from y	$y - 14$
Product of 8 and w	$8w$
Divide z by 6	$\frac{z}{6}$

▶ **Quick Check**

Write an algebraic expression for each statement.

9 Sum of 15 and p

10 Subtract q from 10

11 Product of r and 23

12 Divide s by 11

Evaluating algebraic expressions

Evaluate $4y + 1$ when
a $y = 7$, **b** $y = 10$

a When $y = 7$,
  $4\mathbf{y} + 1$
  $= (4 \cdot \mathbf{7}) + 1$ Substitute.
  $= 28 + 1$ Multiply within the parentheses.
  $= 29$ Add.

b When $y = 10$,
  $4\mathbf{y} + 1$
  $= (4 \cdot \mathbf{10}) + 1$ Substitute.
  $= 40 + 1$ Multiply within the parentheses.
  $= 41$ Add.

▶ **Quick Check**

Evaluate each expression for the given values of the variable.

13 $3x + 5$ when $x = 9$ and $x = 12$

14 $28 - 4y$ when $y = 4$ and $y = 7$

Plotting points on a coordinate plane

Plot points $A(2, 4)$ and $B(3, 2)$ on a coordinate plane.

To locate point $A(2, 4)$, move 2 units to the right of the y-axis and 4 units above the x-axis. Then, mark the point with a dot.

To locate point $B(3, 2)$, move 3 units to the right of the y-axis and 2 units above the x-axis. Then, mark the point with a dot.

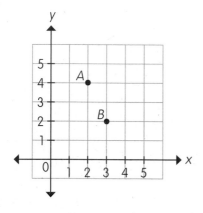

▶ **Quick Check**

Plot the points on the coordinate plane.

15 $K(2, 1)$, $L(3, 3)$, $M(0, 6)$, and $N(7, 5)$

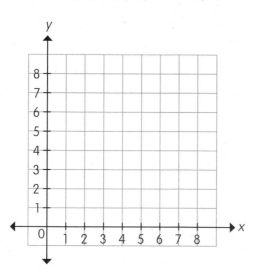

Solving Algebraic Equations

Learning Objective:
• Solve equations in one variable.

New Vocabulary
algebraic equation
solution

THINK

If $x + \frac{1}{3} = \frac{1}{2}$, find the value of $\frac{2}{5}x$.

ENGAGE

Look at the balance.

Key: = 8 lb

How much does the tortoise weigh? Explain to your partner.

LEARN Use substitution to solve simple

1 The figure shows a balance scale. Find the value of x such that the left side balances the right side.

$x + 5$ 8

represents 1 counter.

x represents x counters.

There are $(x + 5)$ counters on the left side.
There are 8 counters on the right side.

Since the beam is balanced,
$x + 5 = 8$.
$x + 5 = 8$ is called an equation.

We can think of an equation using the idea of a balance scale, where the left side is always balanced by the right side.

To solve the equation, we need to find the value of x that makes $x + 5 = 8$ true.

If $x = 1$,　$x + 5 = 1 + 5$
　　　　　$= 6$　　　　$(\neq 8)$

If $x = 2$,　$x + 5 = 2 + 5$
　　　　　$= 7$　　　　$(\neq 8)$

If $x = 3$,　$x + 5 = 3 + 5$
　　　　　$= 8$

The equation $x + 5 = 8$ holds true when $x = 3$.
$x = 3$ gives the solution of the equation $x + 5 = 8$.

What number do you add to 5 to get 8? The answer is 3, so the only solution of the equation $x + 5 = 8$ is 3.

2 Solve the equation $3x = 12$.

The equation $3x = 12$ can be represented on a balance scale:

represents 1 counter.
$\boxed{x}$ represents x counters.

To solve the equation, we need to find the value of x that makes $3x = 12$ true.

If $x = 1$,　$3x = 3 \cdot 1$
　　　　　$= 3$　　　　$(\neq 12)$

If $x = 2$,　$3x = 3 \cdot 2$
　　　　　$= 6$　　　　$(\neq 12)$

If $x = 4$,　$3x = 3 \cdot 4$
　　　　　$= 12$

The equation $3x = 12$ holds true when $x = 4$.
$x = 4$ gives the solution of the equation $3x = 12$.

The equation $3x = 12$ has only one solution, $x = 4$. The equation does not hold true for other values of x.

TRY Practice using substitution to solve simple algebraic equations

Solve each equation using the substitution method.

1 $x + 3 = 7$

If $x = 1$, $x + 3 = $ _____ $ + 3$

= _____   ($\bigcirc$ 7)

If $x = 2$, $x + 3 = $ _____ $ + 3$

= _____   ($\bigcirc$ 7)

If $x = 4$, $x + 3 = $ _____ $ + 3$

= _____

$x + 3 = 7$ is true when $x = $ _____.

2 $p + 6 = 13$

3 $r + 4 = 12$

4 $k - 10 = 7$

5 $2m = 6$

6 $4n = 20$

7 $\frac{1}{5}z = 3$

ENGAGE

Consider ♡ + 4 = 7.
What is the number represented by ♡?
Explain how you can find the answer in two ways.

LEARN Solve algebraic equations involving addition or subtraction

1 Solve the equation $x + 6 = 9$.

The equation $x + 6 = 9$ can be represented on a balance scale:

■ represents 1 counter.
[x] represents x counters.

To have only x counters on the left side and to balance the scale, we remove 6 counters from each side.

So, we can summarize the step above as:

$$x + 6 = 9$$
$$x + 6 - 6 = 9 - 6 \quad \text{Subtract 6 from both sides.}$$
$$x = 3$$

$x = 3$ gives the solution of the equation $x + 6 = 9$.

Check

Substitute 3 for the value of x into the equation.

$$x + 6 = 3 + 6$$
$$= 9$$

When $x = 3$, the equation $x + 6 = 9$ holds true.
$x = 3$ gives the solution.

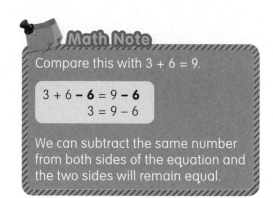

Math Note

Compare this with $3 + 6 = 9$.

$$3 + 6 - 6 = 9 - 6$$
$$3 = 9 - 6$$

We can subtract the same number from both sides of the equation and the two sides will remain equal.

2 Solve the equation $6 = x - 3$.

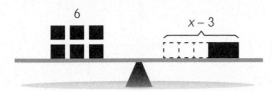
6

$x - 3$

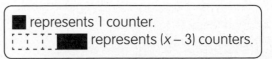
■ represents 1 counter.
⌐ ⌐ ⌐ ■ represents $(x - 3)$ counters.

$6 = x - 3$
$6 + 3 = x - 3 + 3$ Add 3 to both sides.
$9 = x$
$x = 9$

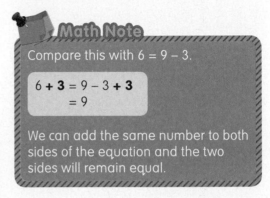
Math Note

Compare this with $6 = 9 - 3$.

$6 + 3 = 9 - 3 + 3$
$= 9$

We can add the same number to both sides of the equation and the two sides will remain equal.

Check

Substitute 9 for the value of x into the equation.

$6 = x - 3$
$= 9 - 3$
$= 6$

When $x = 9$, the equation $6 = x - 3$ holds true.
$x = 9$ gives the solution.

TRY Practice solving algebraic equations involving addition or subtraction

Solve each equation.

1 $x + 8 = 19$

$x + 8 = 19$

$x + 8 \bigcirc \underline{\hspace{2cm}} = 19 \bigcirc \underline{\hspace{2cm}}$

$x = \underline{\hspace{2cm}}$

2 $f + 5 = 14$

3 $26 = g + 11$

4 $w - 6 = 10$

5 $z - 9 = 21$

ENGAGE

a Twice a given number is 6. Find the number.
Explain your thinking using algebra tiles.

b Show different groups of tiles that make 6.
Write an equation for each way.

LEARN Solve algebraic equations involving multiplication or division

1 Solve the equation $2x = 12$.

The equation $2x = 12$ can be represented on a balance scale:

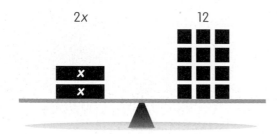

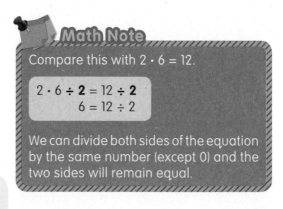

■ represents 1 counter.
[x] represents x counters.

To have only x counters on the left side and to balance the scale, we divide the number of counters on each side by 2.

So, we can summarize the steps above as:

$$2x = 12$$
$$2x \div \mathbf{2} = 12 \div \mathbf{2} \qquad \text{Divide both sides by 2.}$$
$$x = 6$$

$x = 6$ gives the solution of the equation $2x = 12$.

Math Note

Compare this with $2 \cdot 6 = 12$.

$$2 \cdot 6 \div \mathbf{2} = 12 \div \mathbf{2}$$
$$6 = 12 \div 2$$

We can divide both sides of the equation by the same number (except 0) and the two sides will remain equal.

Check

Substitute 6 for the value of x into the equation.

$$2x = 2 \cdot 6$$
$$= 12$$

When $x = 6$, the equation $2x = 12$ holds true.
$x = 6$ gives the solution.

© 2020 Marshall Cavendish Education Pte Ltd

2 Solve the equation $\frac{y}{3} = 4$.

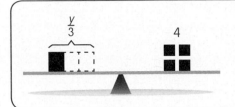

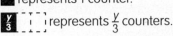 represents 1 counter.

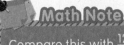 represents $\frac{y}{3}$ counters.

$$\frac{y}{3} = 4$$

$$\frac{y}{3} \cdot \mathbf{3} = 4 \cdot \mathbf{3} \qquad \text{Multiply both sides by 3.}$$

$$y = 12$$

$y = 12$ gives the solution of the equation $\frac{y}{3} = 4$.

Math Note

Compare this with $\frac{12}{3} = 4$.

$$\frac{12}{3} \cdot \mathbf{3} = 4 \cdot \mathbf{3}$$
$$12 = 4 \cdot 3$$

We can multiply both sides of the equation by the same number and the two sides will remain equal.

Check

Substitute 12 for the value of y into the equation.

$$\frac{y}{3} = \frac{12}{3}$$
$$= 4$$

When $y = 12$, the equation $\frac{y}{3} = 4$ holds true.

$y = 12$ gives the solution.

TRY Practice solving algebraic equations involving multiplication or division

Solve each equation.

1 $3x = 27$

$$3x = 27$$

$3x \bigcirc \underline{\hspace{2cm}} = 27 \bigcirc \underline{\hspace{2cm}}$

$$x = \underline{\hspace{2cm}}$$

2 $6a = 42$

3 $65 = 13b$

4 $\frac{m}{8} = 9$

5 $12 = \frac{n}{7}$

ENGAGE

Owen said that solving $x + 1 = 3$ can help you to solve $x + \frac{1}{5} = \frac{3}{5}$.
Do you agree or disagree? Explain your thinking.

LEARN Solve algebraic equations involving fractions

1. Solve the equation $x + \frac{1}{10} = \frac{3}{10}$. Express your answer in simplest form.

$$x + \frac{1}{10} = \frac{3}{10}$$

$$x + \frac{1}{10} - \mathbf{\frac{1}{10}} = \frac{3}{10} - \mathbf{\frac{1}{10}}$$ Subtract $\frac{1}{10}$ from both sides.

$$x = \frac{2}{10}$$ Simplify.

$$= \frac{1}{5}$$

Decide on an operation to use. Since $\frac{1}{10}$ was added to x, we need to subtract $\frac{1}{10}$ from each side of the equation.

2. Solve the equation $3y = \frac{2}{3}$. Express your answer in simplest form.

$$3y = \frac{2}{3}$$

$$3y \div \mathbf{3} = \frac{2}{3} \div \mathbf{3}$$ Divide both sides by 3.

$$y = \frac{2}{3} \cdot \frac{1}{3}$$ Multiply by the reciprocal of the divisor.

$$= \frac{2}{9}$$

Decide on an operation to use. Since y was multiplied by 3, divide each side of the equation by 3.

TRY Practice solving algebraic equations involving fractions

Solve each equation. Express each answer in simplest form.

1. $x + \frac{3}{7} = \frac{5}{7}$

$$x + \frac{3}{7} = \frac{5}{7}$$

$$x + \frac{3}{7} \bigcirc \rule{2cm}{0.4pt} = \frac{5}{7} \bigcirc \rule{2cm}{0.4pt}$$

$$x = \rule{2cm}{0.4pt}$$

2. $k + \frac{1}{8} = \frac{7}{8}$

3. $4p = \frac{3}{4}$

INDEPENDENT PRACTICE

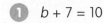

Solve each equation using the substitution method.

1 $b + 7 = 10$

2 $17 = e + 9$

3 $k - 4 = 11$

4 $42 = 3p$

5 $8t = 56$

6 $\frac{1}{4}v = 5$

Solve each equation using the concept of balancing.

7 $k + 12 = 23$

8 $x - 8 = 17$

9 $24 = f - 16$

10 $5j = 75$

11 $81 = 9m$

12 $\frac{r}{6} = 11$

Solve each equation using the concept of balancing. Express each answer in simplest form.

13 $\frac{5}{6} = c + \frac{1}{6}$

14 $h + \frac{5}{14} = \frac{11}{14}$

15 $q - \frac{3}{10} = \frac{7}{10}$

16 $7k = \frac{4}{7}$

17 $\frac{5}{12} = 5d$

18 $\frac{1}{2}x = \frac{1}{4}$

19 $\frac{8}{9} = \frac{1}{3}f$

20 $r + 2.1 = 4.7$

21 $9.9 = x + 5.4$

22 $11.2 = f - 1.8$

23 $j - 3.7 = 20.4$

24 $4w = 6.8$

25 $13.9 = 2.5z$

26 $x + \frac{1}{2} = 1\frac{3}{4}$

27 $e - \frac{18}{11} = 1\frac{6}{11}$

Solve.

28 Find five pairs of whole numbers, such that when they are inserted into the equation below, the solution of the equation is 3.

$$x + \boxed{\ ?\ } = \boxed{\ ?\ }$$

29 Find five pairs of whole numbers, such that when they are inserted into the equation below, the solution of the equation is $\frac{2}{5}$.

$$\boxed{\ ?\ }x = \boxed{\ ?\ }$$

Writing Linear Equations

Learning Objectives:
• Express the relationship between two quantities as a linear equation.
• Use a table or graph to represent a linear equation.

New Vocabulary
linear equation
independent variable
dependent variable

THINK

At a shop, a sales tax rate of 7 percent is charged based on the cost of each item purchased. Use a graph to show the sales tax payable in dollars for five items, each costing less than $100.

ENGAGE

Draw an equilateral triangle and label its sides. Each side of the triangle is s centimeters long. The perimeter of the triangle is p centimeters. How do you express p in terms of s? Discuss.

LEARN Write a ~~linear equation~~ to express the relationship between two quantities

① Jacob is x years old now. Jenna is 10 years older than him now. If Jenna is y years old, write an equation that relates their ages.

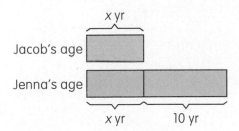

From the bar model, an expression for Jenna's age is $(x + 10)$ years.

Since it is given that Jenna is y years old, we can write an equation relating the two expressions that represent her age.

$$y = x + 10$$

The equation $y = x + 10$ is called a linear equation.

> In the equation, x is called the independent variable and y is called the dependent variable because the value of y depends on the value of x.
>
> Writing y as an expression using x is called expressing y in terms of x.

2. A rhombus has sides of length *r* centimeters. If the perimeter of the rhombus is *P* centimeters, express *P* in terms of *r*.

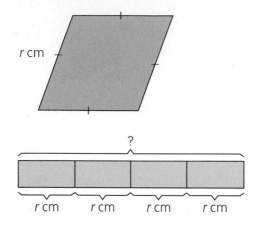

r cm

> Expressing *P* in terms of *r* means that *r* is the independent variable, and *P* is the dependent variable.

?

r cm   *r* cm   *r* cm   *r* cm

From the bar model, the perimeter of the rhombus = $r + r + r + r$
$$= 4r \text{ cm.}$$

Since the perimeter of the rhombus is *P* centimeters, we can write $P = 4r$.

TRY Practice writing a linear equation to express the relationship between two quantities

Fill in each blank.

1. Isaac has *h* baseball cards. Carlos has 7 more baseball cards than Isaac.

   a Write an expression for the number of baseball cards that Carlos has in terms of *h*.

   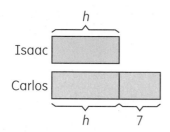

   h

   Isaac

   Carlos

   h   7

   Carlos has _____ baseball cards.

   b If Carlos has *k* baseball cards, express *k* in terms of *h*.

   $k =$ _____ + _____

   c State the independent and dependent variables.

   Independent variable: _____; Dependent variable: _____

Write an equation for each situation. Then, state the independent and dependent variables for each equation.

② Ashley took p minutes to jog around a park. Sofia took 12 minutes longer to jog around the park. If Sofia took t minutes to jog around the park, express t in terms of p.

③ A bouquet of roses costs $30. A bouquet of tulips costs m dollars less. If the cost of one bouquet of tulips is n dollars, express n in terms of m.

$30

④ Orion has 7 boxes of marbles. Each box contains b marbles. If he has c marbles altogether, express c in terms of b.

⑤ A motel charged Mr. Kim x dollars for his stay. Mr. Kim stayed at the motel for 12 nights. If the rate per night for a room was y dollars, express y in terms of x.

ENGAGE

The length of a rectangle is twice its width. Make a table to show five possible values for the length and width. Draw a graph to show how the length and width are related. Examine the graph and explain how they are related.

LEARN Use tables and graphs to represent linear equations

1 The length of a rectangular picture frame is 5 inches longer than its width. Write an equation to show how its width and length are related.

Let w represent the width of the picture frame in inches.
Let ℓ represent the length of the picture frame in inches.

Since the length is 5 inches longer than the width,

$\ell = w + 5$.

Many pairs of ℓ and w values will make this equation true.

Width (w in.)		Length (ℓ in.)
1	+ 5 →	6
2	+ 5 →	7
3	+ 5 →	8
4	+ 5 →	9
5	+ 5 →	10

The length is dependent on the width.

The width (w) is the independent variable, and the length (ℓ) is the dependent variable.

The data can be represented in a table, as shown below. The first row of the table shows values of the independent variable. The second row shows values of the dependent variable.

Width (w in.)	1	2	3	4	5
Length (ℓ in.)	6	7	8	9	10

Use the data in the table to plot the ordered pairs (1, 6), (2, 7), (3, 8), (4, 9), and (5, 10) on a coordinate plane. Connect the points with a line.

© 2020 Marshall Cavendish Education Pte Ltd

Look at the coordinate plane below.
The horizontal axis shows the width of the picture frame in inches.
The vertical axis shows the length of the picture frame in inches.

Dimensions of a Picture Frame

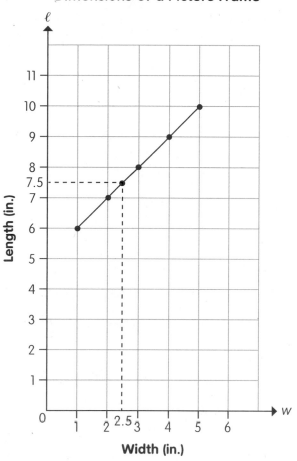

Width (in.)

Use the horizontal axis for the independent variable and the vertical axis for the dependent variable.

The graph of a linear equation is a straight line. It contains all the ordered pairs that make the equation true.

For example, the point (2.5, 7.5) is on the graph of the equation $\ell = w + 5$. We can see that this pair of values make the equation true:

$\ell = w + 5$
$7.5 = 2.5 + 5$

In this situation, the ordered pair (2.5, 7.5) represents the dimensions of a picture frame that is 2.5 inches wide and 7.5 inches long.

6 A rectangle has a perimeter of P centimeters. Its width is b centimeters. Its length is double its width.

a Express P in terms of b.

b Fill in the table to show the relationship between P and b.

Width (b cm)	1	2	3	4	5	6
Perimeter (P cm)						

Use graph paper. Solve.

7 There are x sparrows in a tree. There are 50 sparrows on the ground beneath the tree. Let y represent the total number of sparrows in the tree and on the ground.

a Express y in terms of x.

b Make a table to show the relationship between y and x. Use values of $x = 10, 20, 30, 40,$ and 50 in your table.

c Graph the relationship between y and x on a coordinate plane.

8 Every month, Mr. Lopez spends 60 percent of what he earns and saves the rest. Mr. Lopez earns n dollars and saves r dollars each month.

a Express r in terms of n.

b Make a table to show the relationship between r and n. Use values of $n = 100, 200, 400,$ and 500 in your table.

c Graph the relationship between n and r on a coordinate plane.

d The point (287.5, 115) is on the line you drew in c. What does the point represent? Explain.

9 The side length of a square is t inches. The perimeter of the square is z inches.

a Express z in terms of t.

b Make a table to show the relationship between z and t. Use whole number values of t from 1 to 10.

c Graph the relationship between z and t on a coordinate plane.

d Use your graph to find the perimeter of the square when the length is 3.5 inches and 7.5 inches.

3 Real-World Problems: Equations

Learning Objective:
• Solve real-world problems by writing equations.

THINK

Evan ran at an average speed of 3.5 meters per second for a certain amount of time and then continued to walk at an average speed of 1.4 meters per second for the same amount of time. He traveled a total distance of 137.2 meters. How long did he take to travel the total distance? Write an algebraic equation for the problem and solve it.

ENGAGE

Avery thinks of a number. When she subtracts 12 from the number, she gets 19. Let *n* represent the number Avery thinks of. Draw a bar model to find the number she thought of. Compare your bar model to your partner's.

LEARN Write algebraic equations to solve real-world problems

1. Hugo bought some stamps. His father gave him 12 more stamps and he had 27 stamps in all. How many stamps did Hugo buy?

Let *x* represent the number of stamps Hugo bought.

Hugo bought **some** stamps. His father gave him **12 more** stamps and he had **27** stamps in all.

↓	↓	↓
x	**+ 12**	**= 27**

The equation is $x + 12 = 27$.

To find the number of stamps Hugo bought, solve the equation.

$$x + 12 = 27$$
$$x + 12 - 12 = 27 - 12 \quad \text{Subtract 12 from both sides.}$$
$$x = 15$$

Hugo bought 15 stamps.

Check

When $x = 15$, $x + 12 = 15 + 12 = 27$.
The answer is correct.

2 In a pond, there are 3 times as many guppies as mollies. If there are 48 guppies, find the number of mollies in the pond.

Let m represent the number of mollies in the pond.

There are **some** mollies. There are **3 times as many** guppies **as** mollies. There are **48** guppies.

$$m \qquad \times 3 \qquad = 48$$

The equation is $3m = 48$.

To find the number of mollies in the pond, solve the equation.

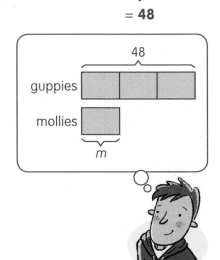

$$3m = 48$$
$$3m \div \mathbf{3} = 48 \div \mathbf{3} \qquad \text{Divide both sides by 3.}$$
$$m = 16$$

There are 16 mollies in the pond.

Check
When $m = 16$, $3m = 3 \times 16 = 48$.
The answer is correct.

Activity **Writing algebraic equations to solve real-world problems**

Work in pairs.

1 Read the word problem. Draw a bar model for the problem.

> There were some people on a bus. 12 more people boarded the bus and there were 21 people in all. How many people were on the bus at first?

2 Use the bar model to write an equation and solve it. Check each other's answer.

③ Repeat the activity to solve each of the following word problems.

a Kayla bought some blouses and T-shirts. She paid a total of $63. The T-shirts cost $29. How much did the blouses cost?

b Brayden and Rachel share $45. Rachel's share is twice Brayden's share. How much does each of them receive?

c Tomas collected some badges. He gave 8 badges to his sister, which was $\frac{1}{3}$ of what he had at first. How many badges did Tomas have at first?

TRY Practice writing algebraic equations to solve real-world problems

Write an algebraic equation for each problem. Then, solve.

1 On Monday, Grace had some leaves in a collection she was making for biology class. After she collected 23 more leaves on Tuesday, she had 41 leaves. Find the number of leaves Grace had on Monday.

Let r represent the number of leaves Grace had on Monday.

$$r + 23 = \underline{\hspace{2cm}}$$

$$r + 23 - \underline{\hspace{2cm}} = \underline{\hspace{2cm}} - \underline{\hspace{2cm}}$$

$$r = \underline{\hspace{2cm}}$$

Grace had _____ leaves on Monday.

2 Adrian thinks of a number. When he adds 17 to it, the result is 45. What is the number that Adrian is thinking of?

3 Emily used 153 yellow beads and some green beads for her art project. She used 9 times as many yellow beads as green beads. How many green beads did she use for the project?

4 James had saved some quarters. He spent 50 quarters, which was $\frac{2}{5}$ of the quarters he started out with. How many quarters did he start out with?

INDEPENDENT PRACTICE

Write an algebraic equation for each problem. Then, solve.

1 Aaron thinks of a number. When he adds 32 to it, the sum is 97. What is the number that Aaron thought of?

2 A baker made some bagels in the morning. After selling 85 bagels, there were 64 left. How many bagels did the baker make in the morning?

3 When a number is doubled, the result is 56. What is the number?

4 Chloe can type on a cell phone 3 times as fast as Megan. Chloe can type 78 words per minute. How many words per minute can Megan type on a cell phone?

5 Miguel spent $\frac{2}{5}$ of his allowance on a jacket. The jacket cost him $12. How much was his allowance?

6 A bicycle store sold $\frac{4}{7}$ of the mountain bikes in the store and 24 mountain bikes were left. How many mountain bikes were in the store originally?

7 Lola has a total of 54 beads. Some are black and some are white. The ratio of the number of black beads to the number of white beads is 7 : 2. How many more black beads than white beads are there?

8 Dominic had a collection of comic books. After 70 percent of his comic books were sold, he had 42 comic books left. How many comic books did he start with?

9 Mr. Perez is 3 times as old as his daughter now. In 15 years' time, the sum of their ages will be 86 years.

   a Find their ages now.

   b How old was Mr. Perez when his daughter was born?

Solarsons of Simple Inequalities

Learning Objectives:
- Use substitution to determine whether a given number is a solution of an inequality.
- Represent the solutions of an inequality on a number line.

New Vocabulary
inequality

THINK

Julia thinks that the solution set for $x > 8$ is the same as that for $x \geq 9$. Explain why you agree or disagree with her.

ENGAGE

Draw a number line to show all the numbers greater than 3.
a Compare two pairs of numbers using the > symbol.
b Can you think of a single inequality that describes your number line? Why or why not?
c Write an inequality that describes all the numbers less than -2.5. What do you notice? Share your observations.

LEARN Determine solutions of inequalities of the forms $x > c$ and $x < c$

1 A bag of tomatoes weighs more than 5 pounds. Find the possible weights of the bag of tomatoes. Then, represent the possible weights on a number line.

Let x represent the possible weights, in pounds, of the tomatoes.

You can write an inequality to show that the bag of tomatoes weighs more than 5 pounds:

$x > 5$

To find the possible weights of the bag, you need to find the values of x that make $x > 5$ true.

When $x = 5.1$, $x > 5$ is true.
When $x = 5.2$, $x > 5$ is true.
When $x = 5.3$, $x > 5$ is true.
         ⋮   ⋮
         ⋮   ⋮
When $x = 100$, $x > 5$ is true.

When $x = 5$, the inequality is not true, since the bag of tomatoes must weigh more than 5 pounds.

The inequality $x > 5$ is true for any value of x that is greater than 5.

Since the inequality has infinitely many solutions, you can represent the solution set on a number line as follows:

> A solution set contains all possible answers to an inequality.

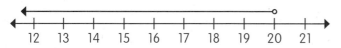

Math Note

The empty circle indicates that the value below the circle is not a solution of the inequality.

The number line above indicates that the inequality $x > 5$ is true for any value of x that is greater than 5. This value can be a fraction or mixed number, decimal, or whole number. For example, $5\frac{3}{8} > 5$, $5.6 > 5$, and $9 > 5$.

2 Consider the inequality $w < 20$.

To find the possible solutions of the inequality, you need to find the values of w that make $w < 20$ true.

When $w = 19.9$, $w < 20$ is true.
When $w = 19.8$, $w < 20$ is true.
When $w = 19.7$, $w < 20$ is true.
      ⋮   ⋮
      ⋮   ⋮
When $w = -4$, $w < 20$ is true.
When $w = -5$, $w < 20$ is true.

The inequality $w < 20$ is true for any value of w that is less than 20.

The solution set can be represented on a number line as shown:

The number line shows values from 12 to 21, with an empty circle at 20.

Activity Writing inequalities of the forms $x > c$ and $x < c$

Work in pairs.

1 The figure shows a balance scale.

Write the equation that this figure represents.

© 2020 Marshall Cavendish Education Pte Ltd

(2) 2 counters are added to the right side. Draw what the balance scale looks like now. Then, write an inequality to represent the relationship between x and the counters on the right side of the balance scale.

(3) 3 counters are then removed from the right side of the balance scale in (2). Draw what the balance scale looks like now. Then, write an inequality to represent the relationship between x and the counters on the right side of the balance scale.

(4) If $y > x$, write an inequality to represent the solutions of $y > x$. Explain how x and y are related using a balance scale.

TRY Practice determining solutions of inequalities of the forms $x > c$ and $x < c$

Use substitution to determine three solutions of each inequality. Then, represent the solution set of each inequality on a number line.

1. $h > 8$

2. $y < 10$

3. $p > 23$

4. $e < 14$

5. $m > 30$

6. $n < 5$

ENGAGE

Draw number lines to show $x = 7$ and $x < 7$. Combining the two number lines, describe in your own words the set of numbers that represents all the numbers on the number lines.

1 Lily needs at least 7 feet of ribbon for her craft project. Find the possible lengths of ribbon that would be enough to complete the project. Then, represent the possible lengths on a number line.

Let p represent the length, in feet, of the ribbon Lily needs.

You can write an inequality to show the possible lengths she needs:

$p \geq 7$

> $\geq$ means "is greater than or equal to."

To find the possible lengths of the ribbon, you need to find the values of p that make $p \geq 7$ true.

> Since Linda needs at least 7 feet of ribbon, this means that 7 is also a possible value of p.

When $p = 7$, $p \geq 7$ is true.
When $p = 7.4$, $p \geq 7$ is true.

When $p = 7\frac{4}{9}$, $p \geq 7$ is true.

When $p = 8$, $p \geq 7$ is true.
When $p = 8.5$, $p \geq 7$ is true.
       :   :

       :   :
When $p = 20$, $p \geq 7$ is true.

The inequality $p \geq 7$ is true for any value of p that is greater than or equal to 7.

Since the inequality has infinitely many solutions, you can represent the solution set on a number line as follows:

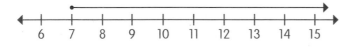

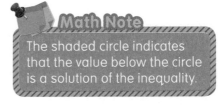

Math Note

The shaded circle indicates that the value below the circle is a solution of the inequality.

2 A ski club is organizing a trip. At least 20 club members have to sign up for the trip to cover the cost of the bus. Write an inequality to represent this situation. Then, state the least possible number of members who have to sign up for the trip to cover the cost of the bus.

Let *w* represent the number of members who have to sign up for the trip.

The **number of members** who have to sign up must be **at least 20**.

w   ≥   **20**

The inequality $w \geq 20$ represents the situation.

The least possible number of members who have to sign up for the trip to cover the cost of the bus is 20.

TRY Practice writing algebraic inequalities to solve real-world problems

Solve.

1 The figure shows a speed limit sign on a highway.

a Let *x* represent the speed in miles per hour.
Write an inequality to represent the situation.

b State the maximum driving speed on the highway.

2 Last Sunday, more than 35 guests attended Jade's birthday party.

a Write an inequality to represent the number of guests who turned up for the birthday party.

b What is the least possible number of guests who could have attended the party?

3 In Ms. Morgan's class, the students are required to summarize a passage in fewer than 50 words.

a Write an inequality to represent the number of words that the students can use to summarize the passage.

b What is the maximum number of words that a student can use?

INDEPENDENT PRACTICE

Solve.

1 Gavin's house is more than 5.4 miles from his school.

    a Let x represent the distance, in miles, between Gavin's house and his school. Write an inequality to represent the situation.

    b Is 5 a possible value of x?

2 A small bus can hold a maximum of 30 students.

    a Let y represent the number of students. Write an inequality to represent the situation.

    b Is 30 a possible value of x?

3 In a science competition, students have to score more than 40 points in order to move on to the next round.

    a Write an inequality to represent this situation.

    b Students are only awarded points that are whole numbers. What is the least number of points a student needs to score in order to move on to the next round?

4 A stadium has a seating capacity of 65,000 spectators.

    a Write an inequality to represent this situation.

    b What is the maximum number of spectators the stadium can hold?

5 To receive a discount coupon at a bookstore, you need to spend at least $50 at the store.

a Write an inequality to represent the amount of money that you must spend in order to receive a discount coupon.

b Emilio spent $45 at the store and his friend Alex spent $55.
Who received a discount coupon?

6 There are 30 teenagers and adults in a gym. If there are at least 16 teenagers, write an inequality to represent the number of adults in the gym.

7 The marbles in a box are packed equally into 6 bags. If each bag has more than 8 marbles, what is the least possible number of marbles in the box?

8 In a competition, each school is allowed to send a team with at least 5 members, but not more than 8 members. 12 schools participated in the competition.

a Find the least possible number of participants in the competition.

b Find the greatest possible number of participants in the competition.

Mathematical Habit 6 Use precise mathematical language

1 Construct a real-world problem involving an equation. Write the equation to represent this situation and solve it.

2 Construct a real-world problem involving an inequality. Write the inequality to represent this situation and state three possible answers.

Problem Solving with Heuristics

1 **Mathematical Habit 7** **Make use of structure**

A rectangular photograph is mounted on a rectangular card. There is a border of equal width around the photograph. The perimeter of the card is 40 centimeters longer than the perimeter of the photograph. Find the width of the border in centimeters.

2 | Mathematical Habit **1** | **Persevere in solving problems**

The price of a box of Brand A crackers was x percent more than the price of a box of Brand B. Sydney paid $55.20 for some boxes of Brand A crackers. If she bought the same number of boxes of Brand B crackers instead, she would pay $7.20 less. What was the value of x?

3 | Mathematical Habit **4** | **Use mathematical models**

k is an integer, and it is a solution of the inequalities $k < 8$ and $k \geq 3$. What are all the possible values of k? Draw a number line to explain your answer.

? How can you use equations and inequalities to describe situations and solve real-world problems?

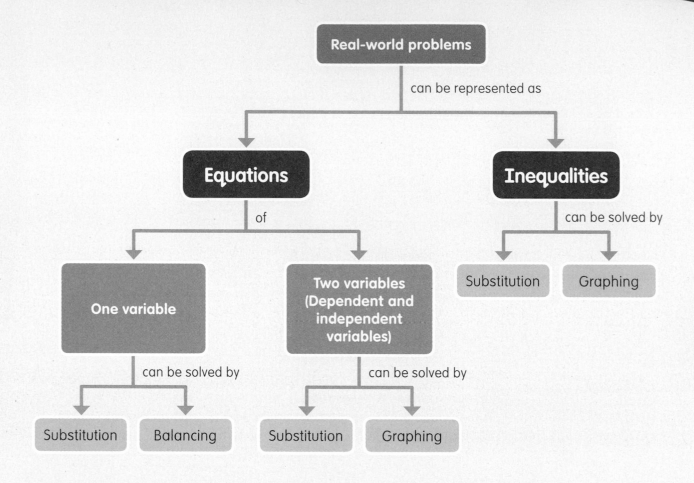

KEY CONCEPTS

• Equations can be solved by substitution, or by adding, subtracting, multiplying, and dividing each side of the equation by the same nonzero number.

  Example: $x + 5 = 14$
  $x + 5 - 5 = 14 - 5$
  $x = 9$

• The solution of an equation is a value, or values, of the variable that makes the equation true.
  Example: $x = 9$ is the solution of the equation $x + 5 = 14$.

• A linear equation with two variables has a dependent and an independent variable.
  Example: $y = x + 8$, where x is the independent variable and y is the dependent variable

• The solution set of an inequality is a set of values that make the inequality true.
  Example: $p > 6$ is true for all values of p greater than 6 such as 7, 7.5 , 8, and so on.

Name: ______________________ Date: ______________

CHAPTER REVIEW

Solve each equation by balancing the equation. Express each answer in simplest form.

1. $x + 8 = 27$

2. $\frac{10}{11} = a + \frac{4}{11}$

3. $f + 3.8 = 9.2$

4. $42 = y - 14$

5. $k - \frac{7}{8} = 2\frac{11}{24}$

6. $n - 2.7 = 13.4$

7. $6h = 84$

8. $75.6 = 7.2r$

9. $\frac{4}{5}p = 10$

10. $9 \cdot \frac{3}{5} = \frac{8}{11}w$

Represent the solution set of each inequality on a number line.

11. $b < 7$

12. $c > 13$

13. $m \geq 24$

14. $n \leq 38$

15. $g > \frac{2}{3}$

16. $h \leq 5\frac{3}{5}$

17. $y < 7.1$

18. $z > 10.4$

Write an inequality for each number line.

19

20

21
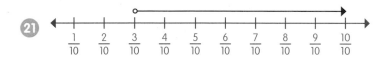

22

Write an equation for each situation.

23 Logan is *x* years old now. His brother is 9 years older than he is now. If his brother is *y* years old, express *y* in terms of *x*.

24 The length of a house is 3 times its width. The width of the house is *f* yards. If the perimeter of the house is *h* yards, express *h* in terms of *f*.

3 Suppose Connor received a total of €4,980 from exchanging U.S. dollars.

  a Write an equation to show that Connor received a total of €4,980.

  b Find the amount of money, in U.S. dollars, Connor exchanged each day. Show your work.

Andrew and Claire exchanged U.S. dollars for another currency. Andrew exchanged USD500 more than double the amount that Claire exchanged.

4 Write an equation to show the relationship between the amount of money, in U.S. dollars, Andrew and Claire exchanged.

5 If Claire exchanged USD1,000, how much would Andrew exchange? If Claire exchanged USD2,000, how much would Andrew exchange? If Claire exchanged USD3,000, how much would Andrew exchange?

a Represent the data in a table.

b Use the data from **a** to plot the points on a coordinate plane. Connect the points with a line.

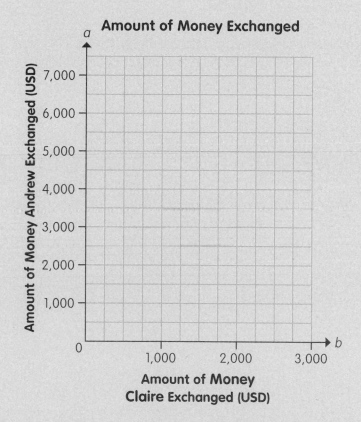

Amount of Money Exchanged

a axis: Amount of Money Andrew Exchanged (USD) — 1,000 to 7,000

b axis: Amount of Money Claire Exchanged (USD) — 1,000 to 3,000

c Use your graph to find the amount of money Andrew exchanged if Claire exchanged USD2,500.

d If Claire exchanged at least USD2,500, write an inequality to represent the situation.

Rubric

Point(s)	Level	My Performance
7–8	4	• Most of my answers are correct. • I showed complete understanding of the concepts. • I used effective and efficient strategies to solve the problems. • I explained my answers and mathematical thinking clearly and completely.
5–6.5	3	• Some of my answers are correct. • I showed adequate understanding of the concepts. • I used effective strategies to solve the problems. • I explained my answers and mathematical thinking clearly.
3–4.5	2	• A few of my answers are correct. • I showed some understanding of the concepts. • I used some effective strategies to solve the problems. • I explained some of my answers and mathematical thinking clearly.
0–2.5	1	• A few of my answers are correct. • I showed little understanding of the concepts. • I used limited effective strategies to solve the problems. • I did not explain my answers and mathematical thinking clearly.

Teacher's Comments

The Coordinate Plane

Have you ever used the maps on your smartphone?

Maps are useful for locating a street in an unfamiliar area. The maps on your smartphone use the Global Positioning System (GPS) coordinates to identify a precise location. The coordinates are usually expressed as the combination of latitude and longitude. Latitude is a measure of the distance north or south of the equator, in degrees. Longitude is a measure of the distance east or west of the equator, in degrees.

When using the maps, you can key in the street name to locate its position. You can also key in the GPS coordinates to locate a specific location along the street.

In this chapter, you will use coordinates to locate points on a coordinate plane.

How do you identify the location of a place on a given map?

Name: _____   Date: _____

Identifying and plotting coordinates

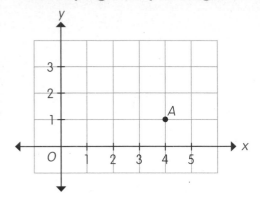

The coordinates of O, the origin, are (0, 0).

To find the location of Point A, move **4** units to the right on the x-axis, and **1** unit up on the y-axis.

The coordinates of A are (**4**, **1**).

▶ Quick Check

Use the coordinate plane below.

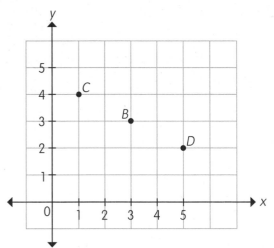

1 Give the coordinates of Points B, C, and D.

Use graph paper. Plot the points on a coordinate plane.

2 P (3, 2), Q (2, 3), and R (0, 4)

Representing negative numbers on a number line

Negative numbers are numbers less than zero.

−2, −10, −23, and −134 are examples of negative numbers.

Negative numbers are found to the left of zero on the number line.

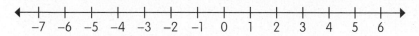

▶ Quick Check

Draw a horizontal number line to represent each set of numbers.

3 −8, −6, −3, 0, 2

4 −15, −11, −9, −7, −2

Recognizing and writing the absolute value of a number

The absolute value of a number is the distance from itself to 0 on the number line. It is always positive or zero.

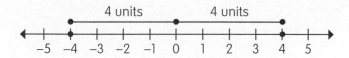

−4 is 4 units away from 0. Its absolute value is 4.
Similarly, the absolute value of 4 is also 4.
You can write $|-4| = 4$, and $|4| = 4$.

▶ Quick Check

Write the absolute value of each number.

5 11

6 −16

7 −21

Identifying special polygons

Polygons are closed plane figures formed by three or more line segments. Here are some polygons.

triangle   quadrilateral   pentagon   hexagon

▶ **Quick Check**

Identify and write the name of each figure.

8   9    10

Finding the perimeter of a figure by adding up all its sides

The perimeter of a figure is the distance around it.

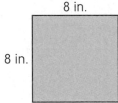

The figure shows a square. Each side of the square is 8 inches long.

Perimeter of the square = 8 + 8 + 8 + 8
= 32 in.

▶ **Quick Check**

Find the perimeter of each figure.

11 Figure *ABC* is a right triangle.

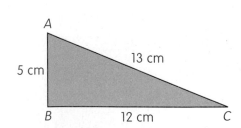

12 Figure *DEFG* is a rectangle.

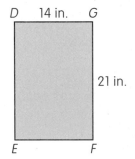

1 Points on a Coordinate Plane

Learning Objectives:
• Name and locate points on a coordinate plane.
• Draw and identify polygons on a coordinate plane.

THINK

Three points are plotted on a coordinate plane as shown on the right.

What are the coordinates of the fourth point, *P*, given that all the four points can be connected to form a rectangle? What are the coordinates of Point *P* if you form a parallelogram instead?

What are two possible pairs of coordinates of Point *P* if you form a trapezoid instead?

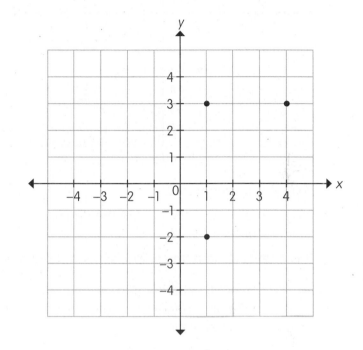

ENGAGE

Audrey plots a point, *M*, on a piece of graph paper. She plots the point 4 units to the right of the origin, and 3 units up.
Michael plots another point, *N*, on the same graph. He plots the point 4 units to the left of the origin, and 3 units down.
Write down the coordinates of the points *M* and *N*. What do you notice about the coordinates of the 2 points? Is there a relationship between the 2 points? Explain your thinking.

LEARN Find the coordinates of points on a coordinate plane

1. A coordinate plane is made up of two number lines that intersect at right angles as shown on the next page.
    The horizontal line is called the *x*-axis and the vertical line is called the *y*-axis.
    The point of intersection, usually labeled *O*, is the origin.

    The *x*-axis and *y*-axis divide the coordinate plane into four parts called quadrants.
    Moving counterclockwise about the origin, the quadrants are named
    Quadrant I, Quadrant II, Quadrant III, and Quadrant IV.

Use the coordinate plane below.

1 Give the coordinates of Points *P, Q, R, S, T, U*, and *V*. In which quadrant is each point located?

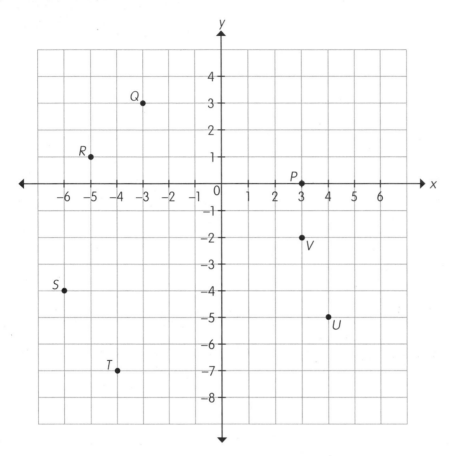

Use graph paper.

2 Plot Points *A* (−4, 3), *B* (3, −4), *C* (5, 0), *D* (0, −5), *E* (−2, −1), and *F* (2, −1) on a coordinate plane. In which quadrant is each point located?

3 Points *P* and *Q* are reflections of each other about the *x*-axis. Give the coordinates of Point *Q* if the coordinates of Point *P* are the following:

a (−6, 2) b (−2, −4) c (4, 5) d (7, −3)

4 Points *R* and *S* are reflections of each other about the *y*-axis. Give the coordinates of Point *S* if the coordinates of Point *R* are the following:

a (−6, 2) b (−2, −4) c (4, 5) d (7, −3)

ENGAGE

Use graph paper. Plot Points $W(2, 3)$ and $X(2, -1)$ on a coordinate plane. Plot two more points, Y and Z, so that all the points can be connected to form a square. What are the possible coordinates of Points Y and Z?

LEARN Draw and identify polygons on a coordinate plane

1. You can connect points on a coordinate plane to form geometric figures.

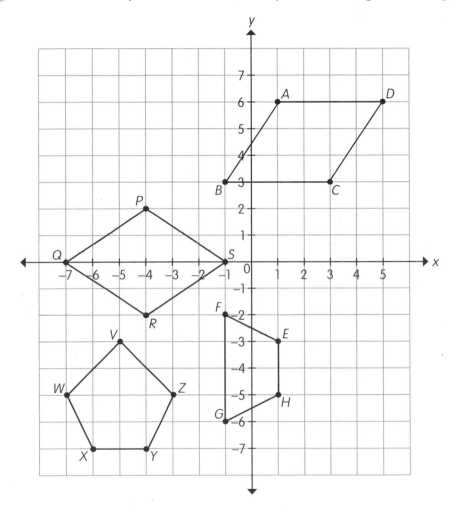

Points $A(1, 6)$, $B(-1, 3)$, $C(3, 3)$, and $D(5, 6)$ are connected to form a parallelogram.

Points $E(1, -3)$, $F(-1, -2)$, $G(-1, -6)$, and $H(1, -5)$ are connected to form a trapezoid.

Points $P(-4, 2)$, $Q(-7, 0)$, $R(-4, -2)$, and $S(-1, 0)$ are connected to form a rhombus.

Points $V(-5, -3)$, $W(-7, -5)$, $X(-6, -7)$, $Y(-4, -7)$, and $Z(-3, -5)$ are connected to form a pentagon.

3 Points A and B are reflections of each other about the *x*-axis. Give the coordinates of Point *B* if the coordinates of Point *A* are the following:

a (4, 1)   b (−2, 3)   c (2, −2)   d (−1, −3)

4 Points *C* and *D* are reflections of each other about the *y*-axis. Give the coordinates of Point *D* if the coordinates of Point *C* are the following:

a (4, 1)   b (−2, 3)   c (2, −2)   d (−1, −3)

Use graph paper. For ⑤ to ⑦, plot the given points on a coordinate plane. Then, connect the points in order with line segments to form a closed figure. Name each figure formed.

5 *J* (−5, 1), *K* (−3, −1), *L* (−1, 1), and *M* (−3, 3)

6 *R* (2, 1), *S* (−1, −3), *T* (4, −3), and *U* (7, 1)

7 *V* (−5, 3), *W* (−5, 0), *X* (−3, −2), *Y* (−1, 0), and *Z* (−2, 2)

Use graph paper. Plot the points on a coordinate plane and answer each question.

8 a Plot Points *A* (−6, 5), *C* (5, 1), and *D* (5, 5) on a coordinate plane.

 b Figure *ABCD* is a rectangle. Plot Point *B* and give its coordinates.

 c Figure *ACDE* is a parallelogram. Plot Point *E* above $\overline{AD}$ and give its coordinates.

9 a Plot Points *A* (−3, 2) and *B* (−3, −2) on a coordinate plane.

 b Join Points *A* and *B* with a line segment.

 c $\overline{AB}$ is a side of Square *ABCD*. Name two possible sets of coordinates that could be the coordinates of Points *C* and *D*.

10 Plot Points *A* (2, 5) and *B* (2, −3) on a coordinate plane. Figure *ABC* is a right isosceles triangle. If Point *C* is in Quadrant III, give the coordinates of Point *C*.

11 Plot Points *A* (0, 4), *B* (−4, 0), and *C* (0, −4) on a coordinate plane.

 a What kind of triangle is Triangle *ABC*?

 b Figure *ABCD* is a square. Plot Point *D* on the coordinate plane and give its coordinates.

Lengths of Line Segments

Learning Objectives:
- Find lengths of horizontal and vertical line segments on a coordinate plane.
- Solve real-world problems involving a coordinate plane.

 THINK

Point *P* is plotted on a coordinate plane as shown.

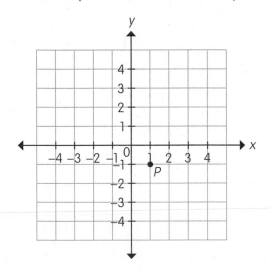

a If Figure *PQRS* is a square and its area is 16 square units and Points *P*, *Q*, *R*, and *S* are located at different quadrants of the coordinate plane, what are the coordinates of Points *Q*, *R* and *S*?

b If Figure *PQRS* is a square and Points *P*, *Q*, *R*, and *S* are located at any three quadrants only, what are the possible coordinates of Points *Q*, *R* and *S*?

ENGAGE

Plot Points *A* (2, 0), *B* (4, 0), *C* (0, 1) and *D* (0, 4) on the coordinate plane below.

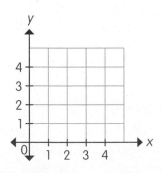

How many units along the *x*-axis is Point *B* from Point *A*?
How many units along the *y*-axis is Point *D* from Point *C*?

1 Find the lengths of $\overline{AB}$, $\overline{CD}$, $\overline{EF}$, and $\overline{GH}$.

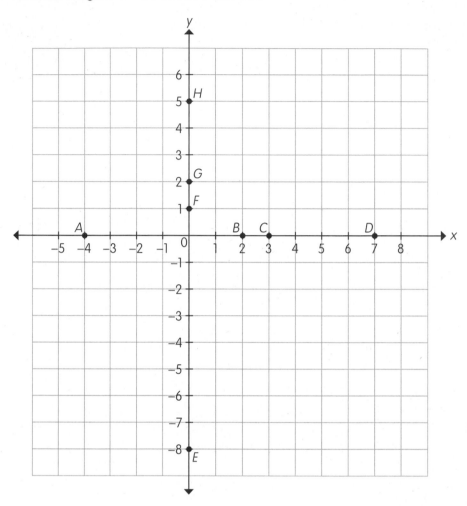

The coordinates of *C* and *D* are *C* (3, 0) and *D* (7, 0).
By counting the number of units from 3 to 7,
the length of $\overline{CD}$ is 4 units.

The coordinates of *A* and *B* are *A* (−4, 0) and *B* (2, 0).
By counting the number of units from −4 to 2,
the length of $\overline{AB}$ is 6 units.

Math Note

Length is a non-negative quantity.
It can be zero or positive.

You can also find the length of $\overline{AB}$ this way.

$$|\overline{AB}| = |\overline{AO}| + |\overline{OB}|$$
$$= |-4| + |2|$$
$$= 4 + 2$$
$$= 6 \text{ units}$$

The length of $\overline{AO}$ is the absolute value
of −4, that is, $|\overline{AO}| = |-4| = 4$ units.

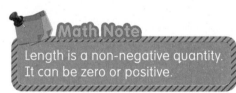

The coordinates of G and H are $G(0, 2)$ and $H(0, 5)$.
By counting the number of units from 2 to 5, the length of $\overline{GH}$ is 3 units.

The coordinates of E and F are $E(0, -8)$ and $F(0, 1)$.
By counting the number of units from -8 to 1, the length of $\overline{EF}$ is 9 units.

Similarly,

$$|\overline{EF}| = |\overline{EO}| + |\overline{OF}|$$
$$= |-8| + |1|$$
$$= 8 + 1$$
$$= 9 \text{ units}$$

So, the length of $\overline{EF}$ is 9 units.

TRY **Practice finding the lengths of line segments on the *x*-axis and *y*-axis**

Use graph paper. Plot each pair of points on a coordinate plane. Connect the points to form a line segment and find its length.

1 $C(3, 0)$ and $D(8, 0)$

2 $E(-6, 0)$ and $F(-2, 0)$

3 $G(-7, 0)$ and $H(1, 0)$

4 $J(0, 5)$ and $K(0, 2)$

5 $M(0, -6)$ and $N(0, -3)$

6 $P(0, -3)$ and $Q(0, 5)$

ENGAGE

a Use a coordinate grid to construct a rectangle labeled *ABCE*, in which one side is on the *x*-axis. What do you notice about the other sides of your rectangle? Compare your rectangle to your partner's.

b Study the points at all the four corners of the rectangle. What pattern do you notice? Share your observations.

LEARN Find the lengths of line segments parallel to the *x*-axis and *y*-axis

1 Find the lengths of $\overline{RS}$, $\overline{MN}$, and $\overline{PQ}$.

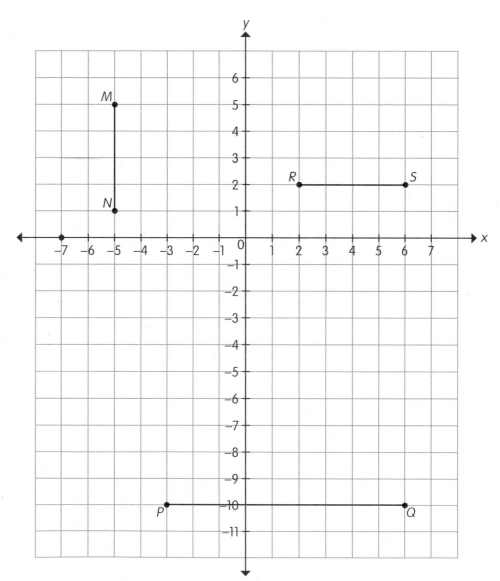

$\overline{RS}$ joins Points R (2, 2) and S (6, 2).
The y-coordinates of Points R and S are the same,
so $\overline{RS}$ is a horizontal line segment.

Using the x-coordinates of Points R (2, 2) and S (6, 2),

$|\overline{RS}|$ = |x-coordinate of S| – |x-coordinate of R|
$\quad$ = $|6| - |2|$
$\quad$ = 4 units

$\overline{RS}$ is parallel to the x-axis.

So, the length of $\overline{RS}$ is 4 units.

$\overline{MN}$ joins Points M (–5, 5) and N (–5, 1).
The x-coordinates of Points M and N are the same,
so $\overline{MN}$ is a vertical line segment.

Using the y-coordinates of Points M (–5, 5) and N (–5, 1),

$|\overline{MN}|$ = |y-coordinate of M| – |y-coordinate of N|
$\quad$ = $|5| - |1|$
$\quad$ = 4 units

$\overline{MN}$ is parallel to the y-axis.

So, the length of $\overline{MN}$ is 4 units.

$\overline{PQ}$ joins Points P (–3, –10) and Q (6, –10).
The y-coordinates of Points P and Q are the same,
so $\overline{PQ}$ is a horizontal line segment.

Using the x-coordinates of Points P (–3, –10) and Q (6, –10),

$|\overline{PQ}|$ = |x-coordinate of P| + |x-coordinate of Q|
$\quad$ = $|-3| + |6|$
$\quad$ = 3 + 6
$\quad$ = 9 units

$\overline{PQ}$ is parallel to the x-axis.

So, the length of $\overline{PQ}$ is 9 units.

TRY Practice finding the lengths of line segments parallel to the *x*-axis and *y*-axis

Use graph paper. Plot each pair of points on a coordinate plane. Connect the points to form a line segment and find its length.

1 *A* (1, −2) and *B* (6, −2)

2 *C* (−1, 3) and *D* (5, 3)

3 *E* (−3, 4) and *F* (1, 4)

4 *G* (−3, 2) and *H* (−3, 6)

5 *J* (−1, −6) and *K* (−1, 4)

6 *L* (5, 6) and *M* (5, 1)

ENGAGE

Use graph paper. Plot Points *W* (2, 8), *X* (2, 2), *Y* (7, 2), and *Z* (7, 8) on a coordinate plane. Connect the points in order to represent a rectangular plot of land *WXYZ*. Each unit on the coordinate plane represents 1 meter. What is the perimeter and area of the plot of land?

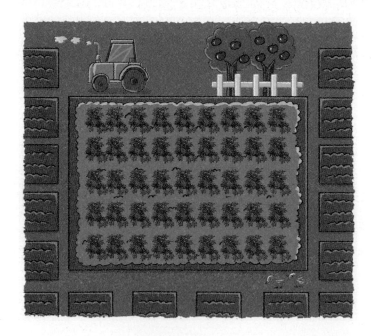

LEARN **Solve real-world problems involving a coordinate plane**

1 A plan of a rectangular backyard is shown. The side length of each grid square is 2 meters.

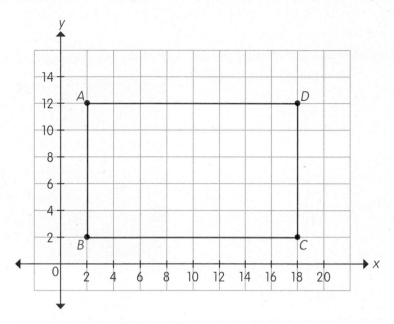

a Give the coordinates of Points *A*, *B*, *C*, and *D*.

The coordinates are *A* (2, 12), *B* (2, 2), *C* (18, 2), and *D* (18, 12).

b Find the length and width of the backyard in meters.

Length = *AD*
   = 18 − 2
   = 16 m

The length of the backyard is 16 meters.

Width = *AB*
   = 12 − 2
   = 10 m

The width of the backyard is 10 meters.

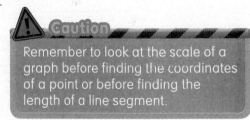

Caution

Remember to look at the scale of a graph before finding the coordinates of a point or before finding the length of a line segment.

c Find the area of the backyard in square meters.

Area = ℓw Write formula.
   = 16 · 10   Substitute.
   = 160 m²   Multiply.

The area of the backyard is 160 square meters.

d Find the perimeter of the backyard *ABCD* in meters.

Perimeter = 2 · (ℓ + w)
      = 2 · (16 + 10)
      = 2 · 26
      = 52 m

The perimeter of the backyard is 52 meters.

e There is a palm tree planted at Point *E* in the backyard at a distance of 12 meters from $\overline{AB}$ and 4 meters from $\overline{AD}$. Give the coordinates of Point *E* and plot it on the coordinate plane.

First, find how many grid squares Point *E* is from $\overline{AB}$.

1 grid square represents 2 meters.
12 m = 12 ÷ 2
    = 6 grid squares

For Point *E* to be in the backyard, the *x*-coordinate has to be 6 units to the right of $\overline{AB}$. So, Point *E* is 1 + 6 = 7 grid squares to the right of the *y*-axis.
The *x*-coordinate of Point *E* is 7 × 2 = 14.

Then, find how many grid squares from $\overline{AD}$ Point *E* is.

4 m = 4 ÷ 2
   = 2 grid squares

For Point *E* to be in the backyard, the *y*-coordinate has to be 2 units below $\overline{AD}$. So, Point *E* is 6 − 2 = 4 grid squares above the *x*-axis. The *y*-coordinate of Point *E* is 4 × 2 = 8.

The coordinates of *E* are (14, 8).

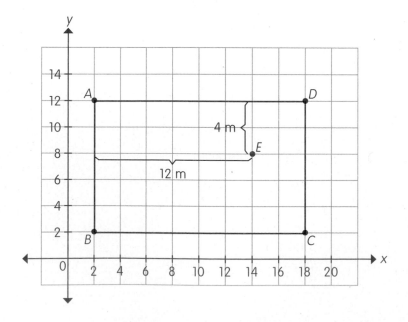

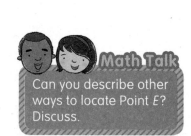

Can you describe other ways to locate Point *E*? Discuss.

© 2020 Marshall Cavendish Education Pte Ltd

TRY Practice solving real-world problems involving a coordinate plane

In the diagram, Triangle *ABC* represents a plot of land. The side length of each grid square is 5 meters. Use the diagram to answer ❶ to ❸.

❶ Give the coordinates of Points *A*, *B*, and *C*.

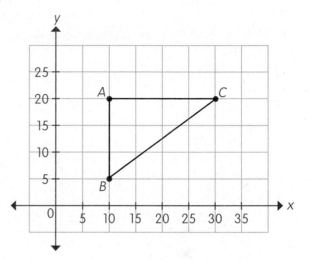

❷ Mr. Martin wants to build a fence around the plot of land. If *BC* is 25 meters, how many meters of fencing does he need?

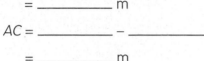

AB = _____ – _____

   = _____ m

AC = _____ – _____

   = _____ m

Perimeter of Triangle *ABC* = *AB* + *BC* + *AC*

             = _____ + _____ + _____

             = _____ m

Mr. Martin needs _____ meters of fencing.

❸ A pole is located at Point *D* on the plot of land at a distance of 10 meters from $\overline{AB}$ and 5 meters from $\overline{AC}$. Give the coordinates of Point *D*.

1 grid square represents 5 meters.

10 m = _____ ÷ 5

     = _____ grid squares

For Point *D* to be on the plot of land, the *x*-coordinate has to be _____ grid squares to the right of $\overline{AB}$.

So, Point *D* is _____ + _____ = _____ grid squares to the right of the *y*-axis.

The *x*-coordinate of Point *D* is _____ × _____ = _____.

For Point *D* to be on the plot of land, the *y*-coordinate has to be _____ grid square below $\overline{AC}$.

So, Point *D* is _____ – _____ = _____ grid squares above the *x*-axis.

The *y*-coordinate of Point *D* is _____ × _____ = _____.

The coordinates of *D* are (_____, _____).

In the diagram, Rectangle *PQRS* represents a parking lot of a supermarket. The side length of each grid square is 4 meters. Use the diagram to answer questions ④ to ⑥.

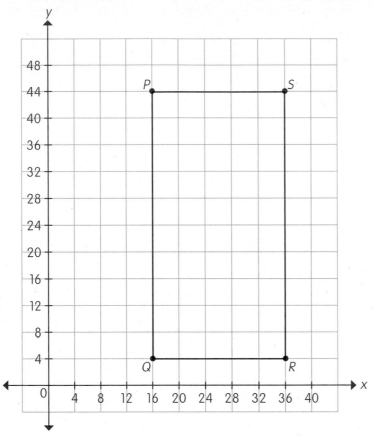

④ Give the coordinates of Points *P*, *Q*, *R*, and *S*.

⑤ The manager of the supermarket wants to build a concrete wall around the parking lot. What is the perimeter of the parking lot?

⑥ The entrance of the supermarket is at Point *T*. It lies on $\overline{PQ}$, and Point *T* is 8 meters from Point *P*. Give the coordinates of Point *T*.

Use graph paper. Plot each pair of points on a coordinate plane. Connect the points to form a line segment and find its length.

1. A (5, 0) and B (8, 0)

2. C (−5, −2) and D (8, −2)

3. E (0, −5) and F (0, 2)

4. G (−6, −3) and H (−6, −8)

Use graph paper. Solve.

5. Rectangle $PQRS$ is plotted on a coordinate plane. The coordinates of P are (−1, −3) and the coordinates of Q are (−1, 2). Each unit on the coordinate plane represents 1 centimeter, and the perimeter of Rectangle $PQRS$ is 20 centimeters. Find the coordinates of Points R and S given these conditions:

   a Points R and S are to the left of Points P and Q.

   b Points R and S are to the right of Points P and Q.

6. Rectangle $ABCD$ is plotted on a coordinate plane. The coordinates of A are (2, 3) and the coordinates of B are (−2, 3). Each unit on the coordinate plane represents 3 centimeters, and the perimeter of Rectangle $ABCD$ is 48 centimeters. Find the coordinates of Points C and D given these conditions:

   a Points C and D are below Points A and B.

   b Points C and D are above Points A and B.

7. Rectangle $PQRS$ is plotted on a coordinate plane. The coordinates of P are (−1, 4) and the coordinates of Q are (−1, −4). Each unit on the coordinate plane represents 1 centimeter, and the area of Rectangle $PQRS$ is 64 square centimeters. Find the coordinates of Points R and S given these conditions:.

   a Points R and S are to the left of Points P and Q.

   b Points R and S are to the right of Points P and Q.

In the diagram, Rectangle *ABCD* represents a shopping plaza. The side length of each grid square is 10 meters. Use the diagram to answer questions 8 to 12.

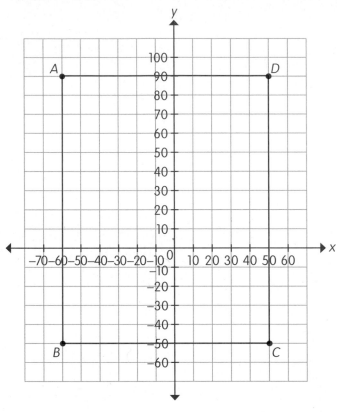

8   Give the coordinates of Points *A*, *B*, *C*, and *D*.

9   Write down the shortest distance of Points *A*, *B*, *C*, and *D* from the *y*-axis.

10   Write down the shortest distance of Points *A*, *B*, *C*, and *D* from the *x*-axis.

11   Find the area and perimeter of the shopping plaza.

12   A man at the shopping plaza is standing 50 meters from $\overline{AD}$, and 40 meters from $\overline{DC}$.

   a   Find the coordinates of the point representing the man's location.

   b   Find the shortest distance in meters from the man's location to $\overline{BC}$.

In the diagram, Triangle **PQR** represents a triangular backyard. The side length of each grid square is 5 meters. Use the diagram to answer questions 13 to 17.

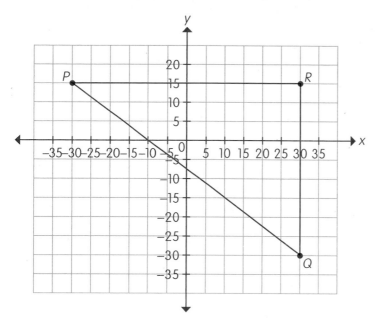

13 A rectangular region *ABCR* in the backyard is to be fenced. Point *A* lies on $\overline{PR}$, and is 35 meters away from Point *P*. Point *B* lies below $\overline{PR}$, and is 20 meters away from Point *A*. Point *C* lies below $\overline{PR}$, and is 20 meters away from Point *R*. Plot and label Points *A*, *B*, and *C* on the coordinate plane. Write the coordinates of Points *A*, *B*, and *C*.

14 If *PQ* is 75 meters, what is the perimeter of the triangular backyard in meters?

15 Find the area of the enclosed region *ABCR* in square meters.

16 Find the perimeter of the enclosed region *ABCR* in meters.

17 If *PQ* is 75 meters, what is the perimeter of the backyard that is not enclosed?

2 A bus uses 1 gallon of diesel for every 6 miles traveled. The relationship between the amount of diesel left in the gas tank, p gallons, and the distance traveled, q miles, can be represented by the equation $q = 96 - 6p$. Fill in the table. Graph this relationship between p and q. Use 1 unit on the horizontal axis to represent 1 gallon and 1 unit on the vertical axis to represent 6 miles.

a

Amount of Diesel Left (p gal)	16	14	12	10	8
Distance Traveled (q mi)	0		24	36	

b How many gallons of diesel are left after the bus has traveled 42 miles?

c After the bus has traveled for 48 miles, how much farther can the bus travel before it runs out of diesel?

d If the bus travels more than 24 miles, how much diesel is left in the gas tank? Express your answer in the form of an inequality in terms of p, where p stands for the amount of diesel left.

3 A kettle of water is heated and the temperature of the water, j°C, after k minutes, is given by $j = 5k + 30$. Fill in the table. Graph the relationship between k and j. Use 1 unit on the horizontal axis to represent 1 minute and 1 unit on the vertical axis to represent 5°C.

a

Time (k min)	0	2	4	6	
Temperature (j°C)		40		60	70

b What is the temperature of the water after 5 minutes?

c What is the average rate of the heating?

d Assuming the temperature of the water rises at a constant rate, what is the temperature of the water after 10 minutes?

e The kettle of water is heated till the water boils. For how many minutes does the kettle need to be heated? Express your answer in terms of k, where k stands for the number of minutes. (Hint: Water boils at 100°C.)

Mathematical Habit 6 **Use precise mathematical language**

Describe how two quantities in real life can be related by a linear equation. Name the dependent and independent variables. Explain how you would use a coordinate plane to represent the relationship.

Problem Solving with Heuristics

Use graph paper.

1 **Mathematical Habit 2** **Use mathematical reasoning**

For **a** to **c**, plot the points on a coordinate plane. Name the figure formed.

a $A(-5, 1)$, $B(-3, -3)$, $C(3, 1)$, and $D(-1, 5)$

b $J(4, 2)$, $K(-2, 4)$, $L(-4, 0)$, and $M(0, -2)$

c $S(-1, 3)$, $T(-3, -1)$, $U(1, -1)$, and $V(5, 3)$

d For each figure in **a** to **c**, mark the middle of each side and connect the points in order. What are the figures formed? Explain your answers.

2 **Mathematical Habit 7** **Make use of structure**

$ABCD$ is a parallelogram. The coordinates of A are $(-5, -4)$, the coordinates of B are $(2, -3)$, and the coordinates of D are $(-3, 1)$. Give the coordinates of Point C.

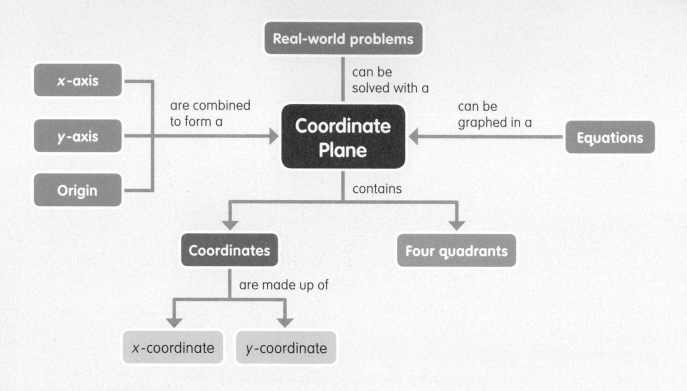

KEY CONCEPTS

- The *x*-axis and *y*-axis divide the coordinate plane into four quadrants. The quadrants are called Quadrant I, Quadrant II, Quadrant III, and Quadrant IV.

- Each point on a coordinate plane can be located by using an ordered pair (*x*, *y*).

- For any point,
  – the *x*-coordinate tells how far to the left or right of the origin the point is relative to the *x*-axis.
  – the *y*-coordinate tells how far up or down from the origin the point is relative to the *y*-axis.

- Points to the left of the *y*-axis have negative *x*-coordinates. Points below the *x*-axis have negative *y*-coordinates.

- A straight line graph is also called a linear graph. A linear equation has a straight line graph.

Name: _____   Date: _____

Use the coordinate plane below.

1. Give the coordinates of Points *A*, *B*, *C*, *D*, and *E*.

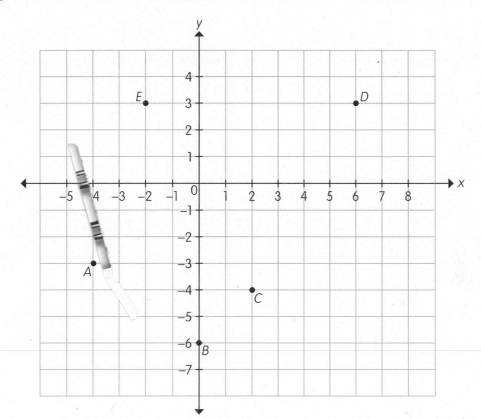

Use graph paper. Plot the points on a coordinate plane. In which quadrant is each point located?

2. *A* (3, 5), *B* (−2, 0), *C* (7, −2), *D* (0, −5), and *E* (−3, −8)

3. Points *A* and *B* are reflections of each other about the *x*-axis.
   Give the coordinates of Point *B* if the coordinates of Point *A* are the following:

   a (3, 6)   **b** (−6, 2)   **c** (5, −4)   **d** (−3, −5)

4. Points *C* and *D* are reflections of each other about the *y*-axis.
   Give the coordinates of Point *D* if the coordinates of Point *C* are the following:

   a (3, 6)   **b** (−6, 2)   **c** (5, −4)   **d** (−3, −5)

Use graph paper. For ⑤ to ⑧, plot the given points on a coordinate plane. Then, connect the points in order with line segments to form a closed figure. Name each figure formed.

⑤ A (0, 1), B (1, 4), and C (−4, 3)

⑥ D (6, 5), E (3, 5), F (3, −3), and G (6, −3)

⑦ J (6, −3), K (4, 2), L (−1, 2), and M (0, −3)

⑧ P (0, 3), Q (−4, 1), R (−4, −3), S (0, −5), T (4, −3), and U (4, 1)

Use graph paper. Plot the given points on a coordinate plane and answer the question.

⑨ **a** Plot Points A (1, −1) and B (7, −1) on a coordinate plane. Connect the two points to form a line segment.

b Points C and D lie below $\overline{AB}$ to form a rectangle ABCD. If BC is 5 units, find the coordinates of Points C and D.

Use graph paper. Plot each pair of points on a coordinate plane. Connect the points to form a line segment and find its length.

⑩ A (−1, 0) and B (9, 0)

⑪ C (−6, −2) and D (−6, −6)

⑫ E (−5, −4) and F (2, −4)

⑬ G (5, −2) and H (5, −5)

The diagram shows the plan of a room. The side length of each grid square is 10 feet. Use the diagram to answer questions ⑭ to ⑰.

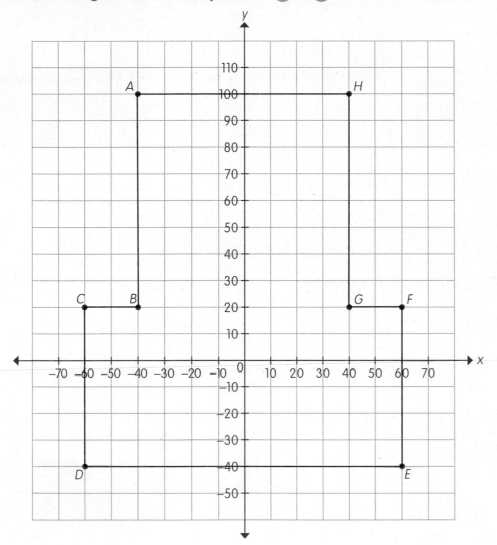

⑭ The eight corners of the room are labeled Points *A* to *H*. Give the coordinates of each of these corners.

⑮ The entrance of the room is situated along $\overline{AH}$. What is the shortest possible distance in feet between the entrance and $\overline{DE}$ of the room?

⑯ Jenna walks across the room from Point *B* to Point *G*, and then walks from Point *G* to Point *H*. Find the total distance, in feet, that Jenna walks.

⑰ Calculate the floor area of the room in square feet.

Use graph paper. Solve.

18 An athlete took part in a race. The distance the athlete ran, v meters, after t minutes, is given by v = 300t. Graph the relationship between t and v. Use 2 units on the horizontal axis to represent 1 minute and 1 unit on the vertical axis to represent 150 meters.

Time (t min)	0	1	2	3	4
Distance Traveled (v m)	0	300	600	900	1,200

a What type of graph is it?

b How far did the athlete run in 3.5 minutes?

c What is the average speed of the athlete?

d Assuming the athlete runs at a constant speed, how far will she run in 8 minutes?

e Name the dependent and independent variables.

19 A truck uses 1 gallon of diesel for every 6 miles traveled. The relationship between the amount of diesel left in the gas tank, r gallons, and the distanced traveled, s miles, can be represented by the equation s = 150 − 6r. Fill in the table. Graph this relationship between r and s. Use 1 unit on the horizontal axis to represent 1 gallon and 1 unit on the vertical axis to represent 6 miles. Start your horizontal axis at 17 gallons.

a

Amount of Diesel Left (r gal)	25		21	19	17
Distance Traveled (s mi)		12	24	36	

b How many gallons of diesel are left after the truck has traveled 30 miles?

c After the truck has traveled for 36 miles, how much farther can the truck travel before it runs out of diesel?

d If the truck travels more than 24 miles, how much diesel is left in the gas tank? Express your answer in the form of an inequality in terms of r, where r stands for the amount of diesel left.

Assessment Prep

Answer each question.

20 Simone knows how to plot Point *A* at (– 4, 3) on a coordinate plane. She needs to plot Point *B* at (– 4, – 3). Where is Point *B* located on the coordinate plane in relation to Point *A*? Write your answer in the space below.

21 Point *L* is shown on the coordinate plane below..

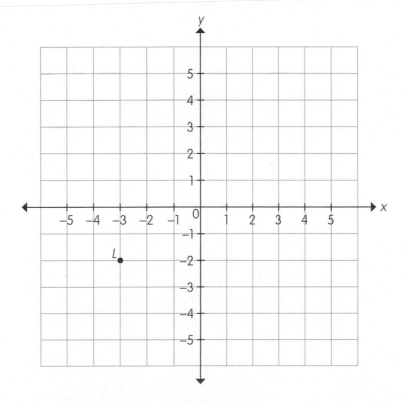

Plot the points that are 3 units from Point *L*, such that they share the same *x*-coordinate as Point *L*. Plot all the points that apply in the coordinate plane. Write the coordinates of the points you plotted in the space below.

22 The coordinate plane shows the locations of three points.

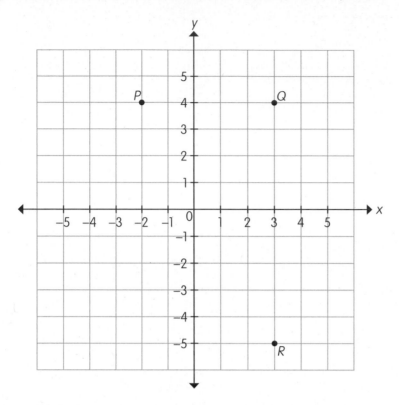

Compare the distance between Points *P* and *Q* and the distance between Points *Q* and *R*. Which is the longer distance, in units? Write your answer and your work or explanation in the space below.

23 Points *A* and *B*, plotted on a coordinate plane, are two vertices of Rectangle *ABCD*. Rectangle *ABCD* has an area of 27 square units. Point *A* is located at $(3, -2)$, and Point *B* is located at $(6, -2)$. Point *C* is vertically above Point *B*. What is the perimeter of Rectangle *ABCD*? Write your answer and your work or explanation in the space below.

Locations on a Map

1 Points *A*, *B*, *C*, and *D* are found on a map. Use the clues to locate the points.

> **Clues**
> - Point *A* is 5 units to the left of the *y*-axis and 5 units below the *x*-axis.
> - Point *B* is the reflection of (5, 6) about the *y*-axis.
> - Point *C* has the same *y*-coordinate as Point *B*, and is 7 units to the right of it.
> - Point *D* is the reflection of (4, 5) about the *x*-axis.

a Plot Points *A*, *B*, *C*, and *D* on the coordinate plane. Label the points with both letters and ordered pairs.

b Connect the points in order with line segments to form a closed figure. Name the figure formed.

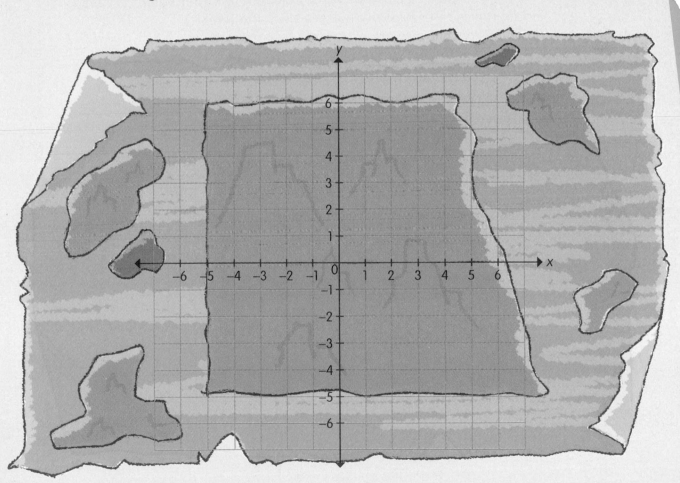

STEAM

Design a Playscape

Where did you like to play when you were in elementary school? Perhaps it was on a local playground. The playground might have swings, slides, monkey bars, and even a merry-go-round.

Today, playscape designers look for creative ways to make fun spaces for children to play. Their plans often include structures that give children choices, such as colorful huts, climbing walls, and complex climbing structures.

Task

Work in small groups to research and design a playscape.

1 Go to the library or go online to learn about uncommon designs for playscapes. Look for examples around the world. Some use recycled materials like cardboard and old tires. Others use things in nature, like tree stumps, tree branches, hillsides, and creek beds.

2 From the examples in 1, come up with an original idea for a playscape. Draw a coordinate grid on a large poster or a sheet of drawing paper. Draw your design on the grid. Mark a point on each structure to use for mapping.

3 Include a playscape legend in your design. Note the coordinates of each structure.

4 Share your map with other groups. Discuss the most creative elements of each playscape and how they might be combined to make play even more fun for children.

Area of Polygons

Have you ever made a mosaic?

A mosaic is a piece of art made by assembling small pieces of colored glass, stone, or other materials. Mosaic art has been around since ancient times and was widely used for decoration.

To create a mosaic, you will need an adhesive surface to hold the mosaic pieces. Preliminary design may be drawn on the surface before fitting the mosaic pieces together. To decide how many mosaic pieces are needed, an artist needs to know the size and shape of each piece. In this chapter, you will learn to find areas of various geometric shapes.

How can you find the areas of various geometric shapes?

Name: _____   Date: _____

Finding the area of a rectangle using a formula

The longer side of a rectangle is called the length. The shorter side is called the width.

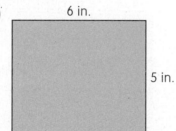

7 cm

4 cm

The opposite sides of a rectangle have the same length. If ℓ is the length and w is the width, the formula for area is Area = ℓw.

Area of rectangle = ℓw
$= 7 \cdot 4$
$= 28 \text{ cm}^2$

The area of the rectangle is 28 square centimeters.

▶ **Quick Check**

Find the area of each rectangle.

1   6 in.

5 in.

2   4 ft

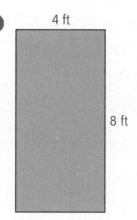

8 ft

Solve.

3   The length of a rectangle is 15 meters and its width is 9 meters. Find the area of the rectangle.

Finding the area of a square using a formula

A side length of a square is 12 meters. Find the area of the square.

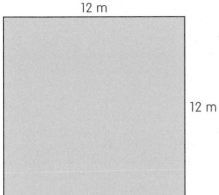

12 m

12 m

The side lengths of a square are all equal. If ℓ represents the side length, the formula for area is Area = ℓ^2.

$$\begin{aligned} \text{Area of square} &= \ell^2 \\ &= 12^2 \\ &= 144 \text{ m}^2 \end{aligned}$$

The area of the square is 144 square meters.

▶ Quick Check

Find the area of each square.

4 4 cm

4 cm

5 9 in.

9 in.

Solve.

6 A side length of a square is 10 feet. Find the area of the square.

Identifying parallelograms, trapezoids, and rhombuses

Figure *ABCD* is a parallelogram. There are two pairs of parallel sides. $\overline{AB}$ is parallel to $\overline{DC}$. $\overline{AD}$ is parallel to $\overline{BC}$.

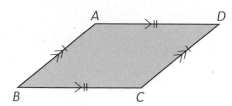

Figure *PQRS* is a trapezoid. There is one pair of parallel sides. $\overline{PS}$ is parallel to $\overline{QR}$.

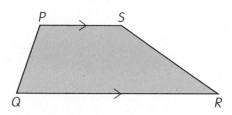

Figure *WXYZ* is a rhombus. The side lengths of a rhombus are equal, and the opposite sides are parallel. $\overline{WX}$ is parallel to $\overline{ZY}$. $\overline{XY}$ is parallel to $\overline{WZ}$.

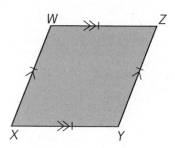

▶ Quick Check

Name each figure and identify the pairs of parallel lines.

7

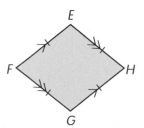

8

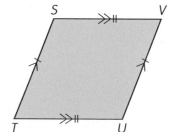

9

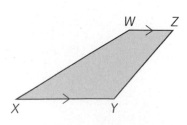

Area of Triangles

Learning Objective:
• Use a formula to find the area of a triangle.

> **New Vocabulary**
> height (of a triangle)
> base (of a triangle)

THINK

The figure is made up of a square and an isosceles triangle.
What is the area of the figure?

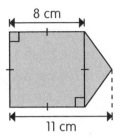

ENGAGE

Copy the three triangles on a piece of graph paper.

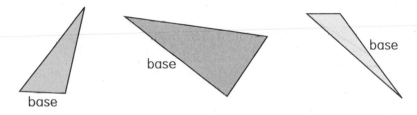

base

base

base

a Mark the height of each triangle, given its base.
b Draw a line segment that is not the height of each triangle, given its base.

LEARN Identify the ▓▓▓▓ of a triangle given its ▓▓▓

1 A triangle has three vertices and three sides.
A, *B*, and *C* are vertices of the triangle.
AB, *BC*, and *AC* are sides of the triangle.

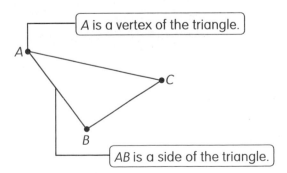

A is a vertex of the triangle.

AB is a side of the triangle.

TRY Practice identifying the height of a triangle given its base

Name the base or height of each triangle.

1

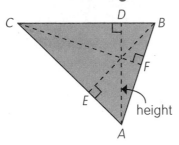

For the height $\overline{AD}$,

the base is _____.

2

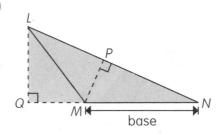

For the base $\overline{MN}$,

the height is _____.

Draw and label the height given the base of each triangle.

3

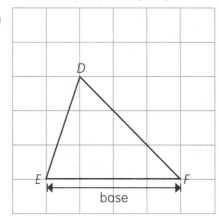

4

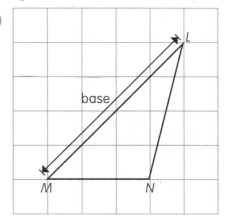

ENGAGE

Form a right triangle with sides 8 units and 4 units on a geoboard. What are two methods to find the area of the triangle? Discuss.

LEARN Find the area of a triangle

1 *ABCD* is a rectangle. In Triangle *ABC*, $\overline{BC}$ is perpendicular to $\overline{AB}$. $\overline{BC}$ is the base and $\overline{AB}$ is the height.

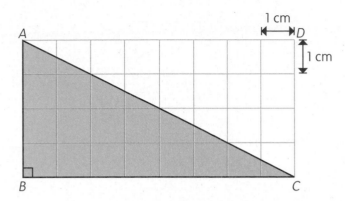

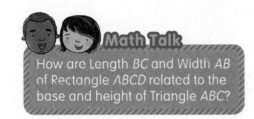

Count the squares to find the area of Rectangle *ABCD*. Count the squares to find the area of Triangle *ABC*. What do you notice?

The area of Triangle *ABC* is half the area of related Rectangle *ABCD*.

Area of Triangle $ABC = \frac{1}{2} \times$ Area of Rectangle *ABCD*

$\qquad = \frac{1}{2} \times BC \times AB$

$\qquad = \frac{1}{2} \times 8 \times 4$

$\qquad = 16 \text{ cm}^2$

Math Talk

How are Length *BC* and Width *AB* of Rectangle *ABCD* related to the base and height of Triangle *ABC*?

Using *b* for base and *h* for height, you can write the formula for the area of a triangle:
Area of triangle $= \frac{1}{2} bh$

Activity Recognising the relationship between the area of a triangle and its related rectangle

Work in groups.

1 Draw each of the following triangles given the base. Label each height.

a Right triangle

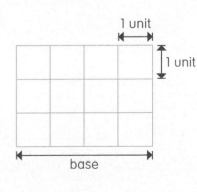

base

b Acute triangle

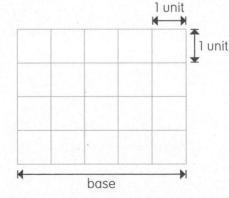

base

c Obtuse triangle

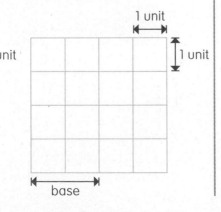

base

② Draw the related rectangles of your triangles in ①. Outline each rectangle in red.

③ Make a copy of your triangles in ①. Cut each triangle to form a smaller rectangle as shown. Example:

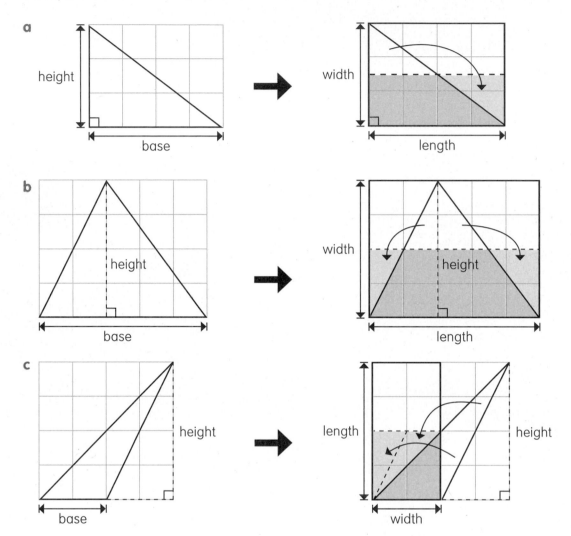

④ Count to find the area of each triangle and the related rectangle in square units. Fill in the table.

	Related Rectangle			Triangle		
	Length (units)	Width (units)	Area (units²)	Base (units)	Height (units)	Area (units²)
a						
b						
c						

⑤ From the table, what do you notice about the base and height of each triangle, and the length and width of its related rectangle?

⑥ What do you notice about the area of each triangle and the area of its related rectangle?

⑦ What is the relationship between the area of a triangle, and its base and height?

TRY **Practice finding the area of a triangle**

Find the area of each shaded triangle.

①

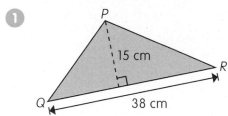

Area of triangle $PQR = \frac{1}{2} \times$ base $\times$ height

$= \frac{1}{2} \times$ _____ $\times$ _____

$=$ _____ cm²

②

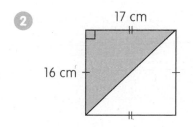

③

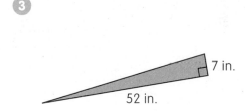

④

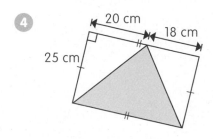

⑤

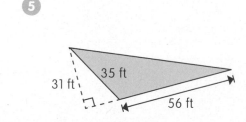

Solve.

6 In Triangle *ABC*, *BD* = 9 meters, *DC* = 10 meters, and *AD* = 18 meters. Find the area of Triangle *ABC*.

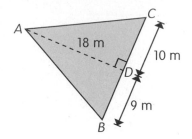

7 In the figure, *KL* = 16 inches, *KM* = 18 inches, and *NL* = 14 inches. Find the area of Triangle *KLM*.

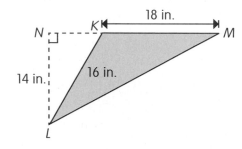

ENGAGE

Fold a rectangular piece of paper to form two triangles.
What are two methods to find the area of one of the triangles? Discuss.

LEARN Find the base or height of a triangle

1 The area of Triangle *FGH* is 46 square inches. Find the height of the triangle.

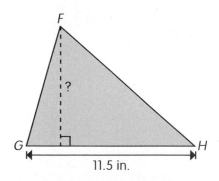

Area of Triangle $FGH = \frac{1}{2}bh$	Write formula.
$46 = \frac{1}{2} \cdot 11.5 \cdot h$	Substitute.
$46 = 5.75 \cdot h$	Simplify.
$46 \div 5.75 = 5.75h \div 5.75$	Divide each side by 5.75.
$8 = h$	Simplify.

The height of Triangle *FGH* is 8 inches.

2 The area of Triangle *XYZ* is 36.5 square centimeters. Find the base of the triangle.

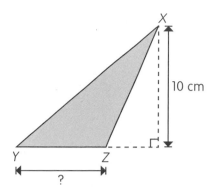

Area of Triangle $XYZ = \frac{1}{2}bh$ Write formula.

$36.5 = \frac{1}{2} \cdot b \cdot 10$ Substitute.

$36.5 = \frac{1}{2} \cdot 10 \cdot b$ Commutative property.

$36.5 = 5 \cdot b$ Simplify.

$36.5 \div 5 = 5b \div 5$ Divide each side by 5.

$7.3 = b$ Simplify.

The base of Triangle *XYZ* is 7.3 centimeters.

TRY **Practice finding the base or height of a triangle**

Solve.

1 The area of Triangle *JKL* is 35 square meters. Find the height of Triangle *JKL*.

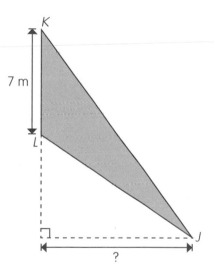

Area of Triangle $JKL = \frac{1}{2}bh$

_____ = _____ • _____ • *h*

_____ = _____ • *h*

_____ ÷ _____ = _____ *h* ÷ _____

_____ = *h*

The height of Triangle *JKL* is _____ meters.

The area of the parallelogram is twice the area of the triangle.

Area of Parallelogram $ABCD = 2 \times (\frac{1}{2} \times$ base $\times$ height$)$
$$= \text{base} \times \text{height}$$
$$= BC \times AX$$
$$= 6 \times 4$$
$$= 24 \text{ cm}^2$$

> Using b for base and h for height, you can write the formula for the area of a parallelogram:
> Area of parallelogram $= bh$

Activity **Finding the area of a parallelogram**

Work in pairs.

Figure $ABCD$ is a parallelogram with base $\overline{BC}$ and height $\overline{AX}$.

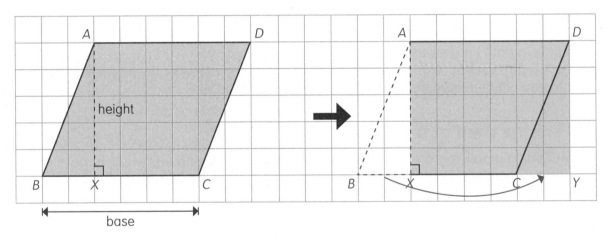

Triangle ABX is cut and moved to the side, where $\overline{AB}$ is placed against $\overline{DC}$.

1 What is the shape of Quadrilateral $AXYD$?

2 What is the relationship between $\overline{XY}$ and $\overline{BC}$?

3 **Mathematical Habit 2 Use mathematical reasoning**
What is the relationship between the areas of Figures $ABCD$ and $AXYD$? Explain your answer.

(4) **Mathematical Habit 7** Make use of structure

The area of a parallelogram is 12 square units. Draw two or more parallelograms that have the same area, with sides that are whole numbers. Label a base *b* and a height *h* for each parallelogram. Compare your answers with your partner's.

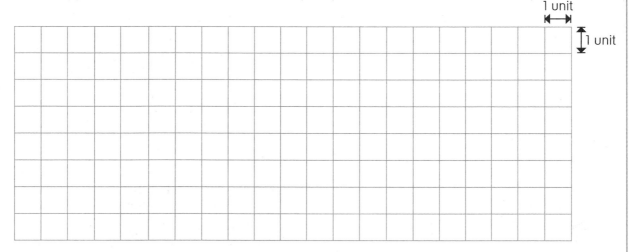

TRY Practice finding the area of a parallelogram

Find the base, height, and area of each parallelogram.

1

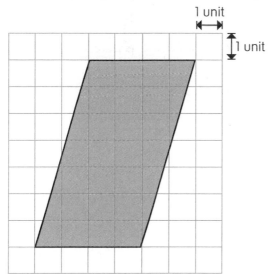

Base = _____ units

Height = _____ units

Area = *bh*

= _____ · _____

= _____ units²

2

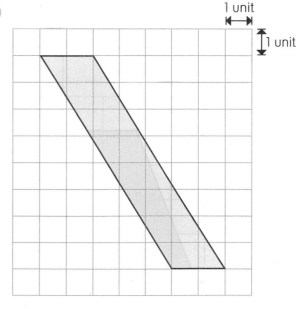

Base = _____ units

Height = _____ units

Area = *bh*

= _____ · _____

= _____ units²

TRY Practice solving problems involving triangles and squares

Solve.

1. Trapezoid *ABDE* is made up of Square *ABCE* and Triangle *ECD*. The area of Triangle *ECD* is 60 square inches. The length of $\overline{CD}$ is 12 inches.

   a Find the height of Triangle *ECD*.

   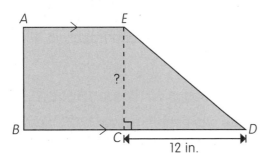

   12 in.

   $$\text{Area of Triangle } ECD = \frac{1}{2}bh$$

   $$\underline{\hspace{2cm}} = \frac{1}{2} \cdot \underline{\hspace{2cm}} \cdot EC$$

   $$\underline{\hspace{2cm}} = \underline{\hspace{2cm}} \cdot EC$$

   $$\underline{\hspace{2cm}} \div \underline{\hspace{2cm}} = \underline{\hspace{2cm}} \cdot EC \div \underline{\hspace{2cm}}$$

   $$\underline{\hspace{2cm}} = EC$$

   The height of Triangle *ECD* is _____ inches.

   b Find the area of Square *ABCE*.

   $$\text{Area of Square } ABCE = \ell^2$$

   $$= \underline{\hspace{2cm}}^2$$

   $$= \underline{\hspace{2cm}} \text{ in}^2$$

   The area of Square *ABCE* is _____ square inches.

   c Find the area of Trapezoid *ABDE*.

   Area of the Trapezoid *ABDE*

   = Area of Square *ABCE* + Area of Triangle *ECD*

   $$= \underline{\hspace{2cm}} + \underline{\hspace{2cm}}$$

   $$= \underline{\hspace{2cm}} \text{ in}^2$$

   The area of Trapezoid *ABDE* is _____ square inches.

ENGAGE

Draw a parallelogram on a piece of graph paper. How many sides must you draw to form a trapezoid? How can you find the area of the parallelogram and the trapezoid? Explain your thinking. List the steps that you took to find the answers.

LEARN Solve problems involving triangles, squares, and parallelograms

1 Trapezoid *PQTU* is made up of Parallelogram *PQRV*, Triangle *VRS*, and Square *VSTU*. The area of Trapezoid *PQSV* is 99 square inches. Find the area of Trapezoid *PQTU*.

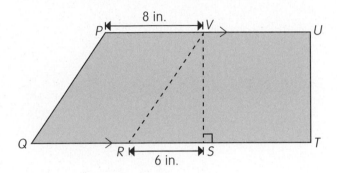

First, apply the formula for the area of a trapezoid to find *VS*.
Area of Trapezoid *PQSV*

$$= \frac{1}{2}h(b_1 + b_2)$$

$$= \frac{1}{2} \cdot VS \cdot (PV + QS)$$

$$= \frac{1}{2} \cdot VS \cdot (8 + 8 + 6)$$

$$= \frac{1}{2} \cdot VS \cdot 22$$

$$= 11 \cdot VS$$

Area of Trapezoid *PQSV* = 11 · *VS*	Write formula.
99 = 11 · *VS*	Substitute.
99 ÷ 11 = 11 · *VS* ÷ 11	Divide each side by 11.
9 = *VS*	Simplify.

Then, find the area of Square *VSTU*.

Area of Square *VSTU* = *VS*²
= 9²
= 81 in²

Next, find the area of Trapezoid *PQTU*.

Area of Trapezoid *PQTU* = Area of Trapezoid *PQSV* + Area of Square *VSTU*
= 99 + 81
= 180 in²

The area of Trapezoid *PQTU* is 180 square inches.

Solve.

1. Trapezoid *ADEF* is made up of Parallelogram *ABEF* and Triangle *BDE*.
   The area of Parallelogram *ABEF* is 84 square meters.

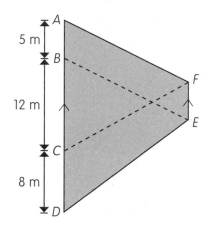

a Find the area of Triangle *BDE*.

Area of Parallelogram *ABEF* = *bh*

$$\underline{\hspace{2cm}} = \underline{\hspace{2cm}} \cdot h$$

$$\underline{\hspace{2cm}} \div \underline{\hspace{2cm}} = \underline{\hspace{2cm}} h \div \underline{\hspace{2cm}}$$

$$\underline{\hspace{2cm}} = h$$

The height of Parallelogram *ABEF* is also the height of Triangle *BDE*.

Area of Triangle $BDE = \frac{1}{2}bh$

$$= \frac{1}{2} \cdot BD \cdot h$$

$$= \frac{1}{2} \cdot \left(\underline{\hspace{1.5cm}} + \underline{\hspace{1.5cm}} \right) \cdot \underline{\hspace{1.5cm}}$$

$$= \underline{\hspace{2cm}} \text{ m}^2$$

The area of Triangle *BDE* is _____ square meters.

b Find the area of Trapezoid *CDEF*.

Parallelogram *ABEF* and Trapezoid *CDEF* have the same height.

Area of Trapezoid $CDEF = \frac{1}{2}h(b_1 + b_2)$

$$= \underline{\hspace{2cm}} \cdot \underline{\hspace{2cm}} \cdot (\underline{\hspace{2cm}} + \underline{\hspace{2cm}})$$

$$= \underline{\hspace{2cm}} \text{ m}^2$$

The area of Trapezoid *CDEF* is _____ square meters.

INDEPENDENT PRACTICE

Label a base, *b*, and a height, *h*, for each parallelogram.

1

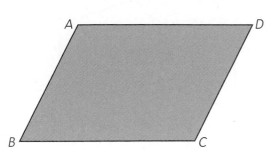

2

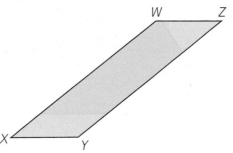

3

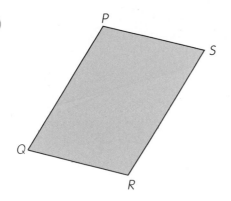

4

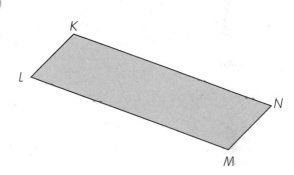

Find the area of each parallelogram.

5

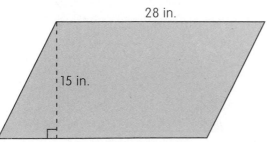

28 in.

15 in.

6

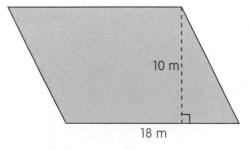

10 m

18 m

The area of each parallelogram is 64 square inches. Find the height. Round your answer to the nearest tenth of an inch.

17

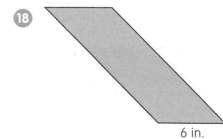

7 in.

18

6 in.

The area of each trapezoid is 42 square centimeters. Find the height. Round your answer to the nearest tenth of a centimeter.

19

5 cm

7.5 cm

20

5.7 cm

10 cm

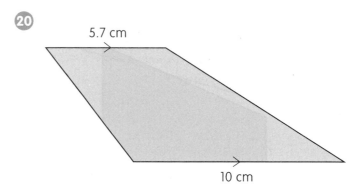

Solve.

21 The area of Trapezoid *ABCD* is 503.25 square centimeters. Find the length of $\overline{BC}$.

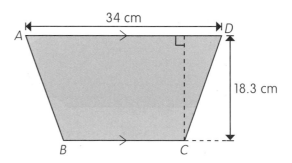

34 cm

18.3 cm

22 The area of Trapezoid *EFGH* is 273 square centimeters. Find the area of Triangle *EGH*.

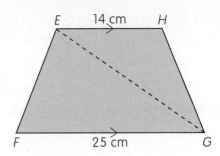

Solve. Use graph paper.

23 The coordinates of the vertices of a parallelogram are *P* (0, 5), *Q* (−3, 0), *R* (2, 0), and *S* (5, 5). Find the area of Parallelogram *PQRS*.

24 Three out of the four coordinates of the vertices of Parallelogram *WXYZ* are *W* (0, 1), *X* (−4, −4), and *Y* (−1, −4). Find the coordinates of *Z*. Then, find the area of the parallelogram.

25 The coordinates of the vertices of Trapezoid *EFGH* are *E* (−3, 3), *F* (−3, 0), *G* (1, −4), and *H* (1, 4). Find the area of the trapezoid.

26 Three out of the four coordinates of the vertices of trapezoid *ABCD* are *A* (0, 1), *B* (−4, −4), and *C* (−1, −4). $\overline{AD}$ is parallel to $\overline{BC}$. *AD* is 6 units. Point *D* lies to the right of Point *A*. Find the coordinates of Point *D*. Then, find the area of the trapezoid.

Solve.

27 Parallelogram *PQRT* is made up of Isosceles triangle *PST* and Trapezoid *PQRS*. Find the area of Parallelogram *PQRT*.

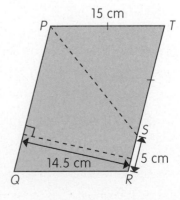

28 Parallelogram *ABDE* is made up of Square *ACDF*, Triangle *ABC*, and Triangle *FDE*. Triangles *ABC* and *FDE* are identical. The area of Triangle *ABC* is 12 square meters. Find the area of Square *ACDF*. Then, find the area of Parallelogram *ABDE*.

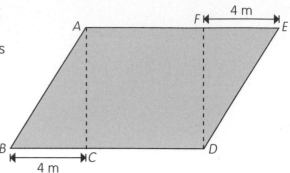

29 Trapezoid *ABDE* is made up of three triangles, and Figure *ABCE* is a parallelogram. Find the area of Triangle *EBC* if the area of Trapezoid *ABDE* is 180 square centimeters.

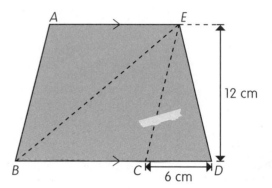

30 Trapezoid *MNRS* is made up of Trapezoid *MNPT*, Triangle *TPQ*, and Parallelogram *TQRS*. The area of Triangle *TPQ* is 84 square feet. The lengths of $\overline{NP}$, $\overline{PQ}$, and $\overline{QR}$ are in the ratio 2 : 1.5 : 1. Find the area of Trapezoid *MNRS*.

Solve. Use graph paper.

31 a Plot Points *P* (−2, 2), *Q* (−2, −2), *R* (−4, −5), *S* (1, −5), and *T* (3, −2) on a coordinate plane. Join the points in order to form Figure *PQRST*.

b Find the area of Figure *PQRST*.

c Point *V* lies on along $\overline{QT}$. The area of Triangle *PQV* is $\frac{2}{5}$ the area of Triangle *PQT*. Give the coordinates of Point *V*. Plot Point *V* on the coordinate plane.

3 Area of Other Polygons

Learning Objectives:
- Divide polygons into triangles.
- Find the area of a regular polygon by dividing it into smaller shapes.

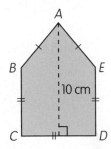

New Vocabulary
kite
regular polygon

THINK

$ABCDE$ is a pentagon, with $AB = AE$, and $BC = CD = DE$. The height from A to $\overline{CD}$ is 10 centimeters. The area of the pentagon is 48 square centimeters. Find the length of $\overline{BC}$.

ENGAGE

Draw a line segment on the figure to divide it into two identical triangles. Then, draw another line segment on the figure to divide it into two different triangles. What do you notice about the triangles? Share your observations.

LEARN Find the area of a ▓▓▓

1. Jada drew a kite as shown below. She divided the kite into two triangles, A and B. Find the area of the kite.

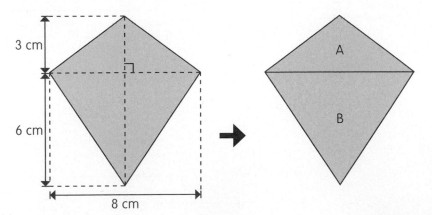

3 cm

6 cm

8 cm

A

B

The area of the kite is the sum of the areas of Triangles A and B.

Math Note
A kite is a quadrilateral with two equal pairs of adjacent sides. The diagonals cut each other at right angles.

Area of Triangle A = $\frac{1}{2}bh$

$= \frac{1}{2} \cdot 8 \cdot 3$

$= 12$ cm²

Area of Triangle B = $\frac{1}{2}bh$

$= \frac{1}{2} \cdot 8 \cdot 6$

$= 24$ cm²

Area of kite = 12 + 24

$= 36$ cm²

The area of the kite is 36 square centimeters.

Math Talk
What is another way to find the area of the kite? Discuss.

TRY Practice finding the area of a kite

Solve.

1 Luis drew a kite as shown below. He divided the kite into two triangles, P and Q. Find the area of the kite.

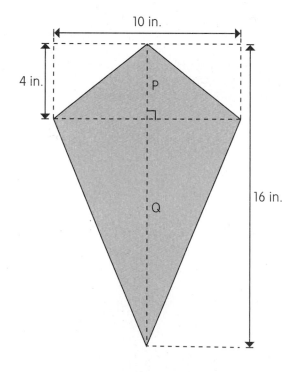

Area of Triangle P = $\frac{1}{2}bh$

$= \frac{1}{2} \cdot$ _____ $\cdot$ _____

$=$ _____ in²

Height of Triangle Q = _____ − _____

$=$ _____ in.

Area of Triangle Q = $\frac{1}{2}bh$

$= \frac{1}{2} \cdot$ _____ $\cdot$ _____

$=$ _____ in²

Area of kite = _____ + _____

$=$ _____ in²

The area of the kite is _____ square inches.

Find the area of each kite.

2

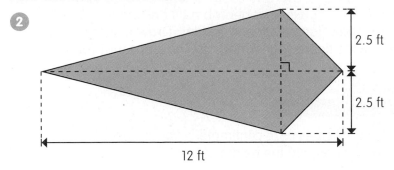

2.5 ft

2.5 ft

12 ft

3

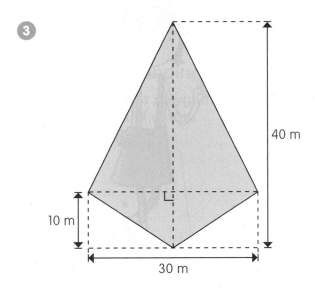

40 m

10 m

30 m

Complete.

3 Brian drew a regular pentagon with equal sides of 6 inches. He divided the pentagon into 5 identical triangles, and measured the height of one of the triangles to be 4.1 inches. Find the area of the pentagon.

Area of each triangle = $\frac{1}{2}bh$

= _____ · _____ · _____

= _____ in²

Area of pentagon = _____ · area of each triangle

= _____ · _____

= _____ in²

The area of the pentagon is _____ square inches.

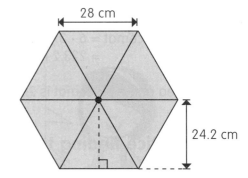

6 in.

4.1 in.

4 Leah drew a regular hexagon with equal sides of 28 centimeters. She divided the hexagon into 6 identical triangles, and measured the height of one of the triangles to be 24.2 centimeters. Find the area of the hexagon.

28 cm

24.2 cm

© 2020 Marshall Cavendish Education Pte Ltd

Use paper cutouts of five different regular polygons. Fold each regular polygon to find the number of lines of symmetry.

a How is the number of sides of a regular polygon related to its number of lines of symmetry?

b Divide each regular polygon into identical triangles. What is the minimum number of identical triangles you could obtain?

c What do you notice about your answers in **a** and **b**?

LET'S EXPLORE

INDEPENDENT PRACTICE

Find the area of each kite.

1

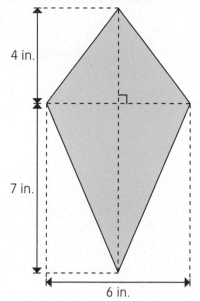

4 in.

7 in.

6 in.

2

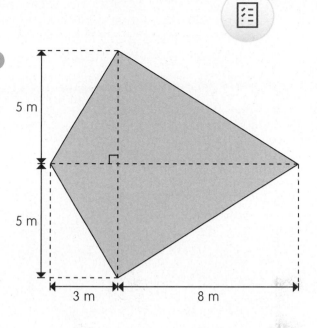

5 m

5 m

3 m

8 m

Divide each regular polygon into identical triangles. Write the minimum number of triangles you could obtain.

3

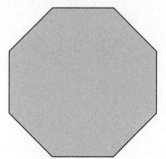

4

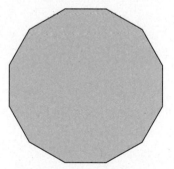

Solve.

5 Ethan drew a regular pentagon with equal sides of 8 centimeters. He divided the pentagon into 5 identical triangles, and measured the height of one of the triangles to be 5.5 centimeters. Find the area of the pentagon.

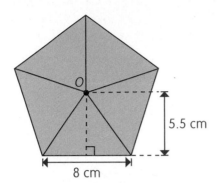

6 Davi drew a regular hexagon. She divided it into 6 identical triangles, and measured the height of one of the triangles to be 4 inches. The area of the hexagon is 55.2 square inches. Find the length of each side of the hexagon.

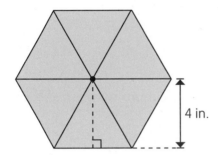

7 A floor tile is in the shape of a regular hexagon. Tristan uses 187.5 floor tiles for a room. The area of the room is 450 square feet. Find the length of each side of the hexagon.

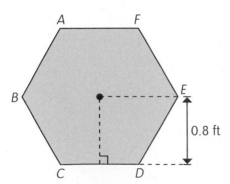

Find the area of each regular polygon.

8 The shaded area is 9.7 square inches.

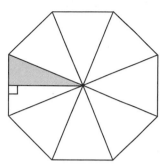

9 The shaded area is 12.8 square centimeters.

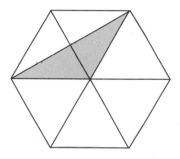

Solve.

10 Suppose you have three identical equilateral triangles. Use a sketch to show how you can make each of the following from two or three of the triangles. Identify the quadrilateral.

a A quadrilateral whose area is 2 times the area of the equilateral triangle

b A quadrilateral whose area is 3 times the area of the equilateral triangle

5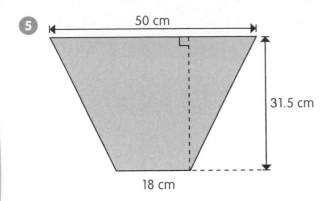

50 cm

31.5 cm

18 cm

6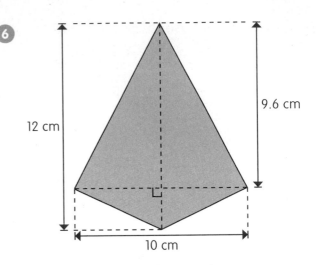

12 cm

9.6 cm

10 cm

Find the area of each shaded region.

7 The area of the regular octagon below is 560 square inches.

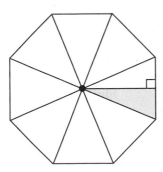

8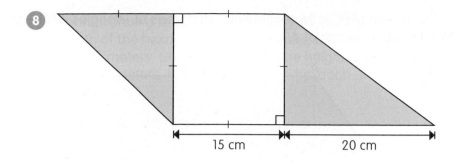

15 cm   20 cm

Solve.

9 Figure *ABCD* is a parallelogram. *BC* is 16 centimeters, *CD* is 12 centimeters, and *AH* is 10 centimeters.

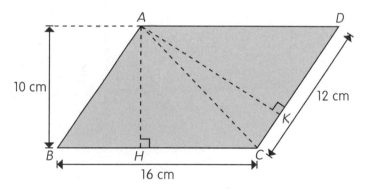

a Find the area of Parallelogram *ABCD*.

b Find the length of $\overline{AK}$. Round your answer to the nearest tenth of a centimeter.

3 The rug maker wants to use less quilted fabrics. Which design, A or B, should the rug maker choose? Explain your answer.

Rubric

Point(s)	Level	My Performance
7–8	4	• Most of my answers are correct. • I showed complete understanding of the concepts. • I used effective and efficient strategies to solve the problems. • I explained my answers and mathematical thinking clearly and completely.
5–6.5	3	• Some of my answers are correct. • I showed adequate understanding of the concepts. • I used effective strategies to solve the problems. • I explained my answers and mathematical thinking clearly.
3–4.5	2	• A few of my answers are correct. • I showed some understanding of the concepts. • I used some effective strategies to solve the problems. • I explained some of my answers and mathematical thinking clearly.
0–2.5	1	• A few of my answers are correct. • I showed little understanding of the concepts. • I used limited effective strategies to solve the problems. • I did not explain my answers and mathematical thinking clearly.

Teacher's Comments

Surface Area and Volume of Solids

How can math help you make candles?

To make a candle, you need some wax, a mold, and a wick. First, melt the wax and pour it into the mold. Then, insert the wick. When the wax has cooled and hardened, wrap the candle in plastic. How much wax do you need? To find out, calculate the volume of the mold. How much plastic wrap do you need? To find out, calculate the surface area of the candle. In this chapter, you will learn to calculate the volumes of rectangular prisms, and the surface areas of prisms and pyramids.

? How can you make use of surface area and volume of prisms to solve real-world problems?

Name: _____   Date: _____

Finding the area of a rectangle, a triangle, and a trapezoid

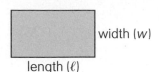
width (*w*)
length (ℓ)

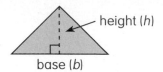
height (*h*)
base (*b*)

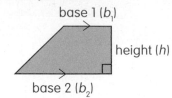
base 1 (*b*₁)
height (*h*)
base 2 (*b*₂)

Area of rectangle	Area of triangle	Area of trapezoid
= length · width	= $\frac{1}{2}$ · base · height	= $\frac{1}{2}$ · height · sum of parallel sides
$A = \ell \cdot w$ or ℓw	$A = \frac{1}{2} \cdot b \cdot h$ or $\frac{1}{2}bh$	$A = \frac{1}{2} \cdot h \cdot (b_1 + b_2)$ or $\frac{1}{2}h(b_1 + b_2)$

▶ **Quick Check**

Find the area of each figure.

1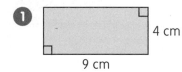
4 cm
9 cm

2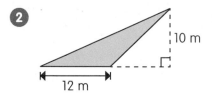
10 m
12 m

3
10 in.
6.5 in.
6 in.

Finding the volumes of rectangular prisms

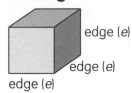
edge (*e*)
edge (*e*)
edge (*e*)

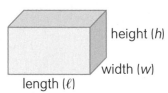
height (*h*)
width (*w*)
length (ℓ)

Volume of cube	Volume of rectangular prism
= edge · edge · edge	= length · width · height
$V = e \cdot e \cdot e$ or e^3	$V = \ell \cdot w \cdot h$ or ℓwh

▶ **Quick Check**

Find the volume of each solid.

4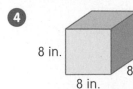
8 in.
8 in.
8 in.

5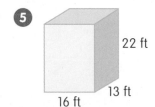
22 ft
16 ft
13 ft

Prisms and Pyramids

Learning Objectives:
• Identify prisms and pyramids.
• Identify the nets of a prism and a pyramid.
• Identify the solid formed by a given net.

THINK

The net of a solid has some faces which are isosceles triangles. Make a sketch of possible solids and then name the solids. How many faces, edges, and vertices does each possible solid have?

ENGAGE

Look around the classroom to find a solid that has 6 flat faces and 12 edges. Compare your solid to your partner's. How are they the same? How are they different? Discuss.

LEARN Describe a solid figure by its faces, edges, and vertices

1 The following figures are solid figures or three-dimensional figures.

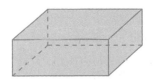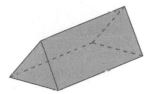

You can classify solid figures by their faces, edges, and vertices.

An edge of a solid figure is a line segment formed when two faces meet.
A vertex is the point where three or more edges meet.

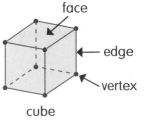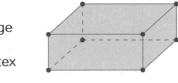

A cube has 6 square faces, 12 edges, and 8 vertices.

TRY Practice identifying the net of a rectangular and a triangular prism

Match each solid with its net(s). Fill in the table.

1

Solid	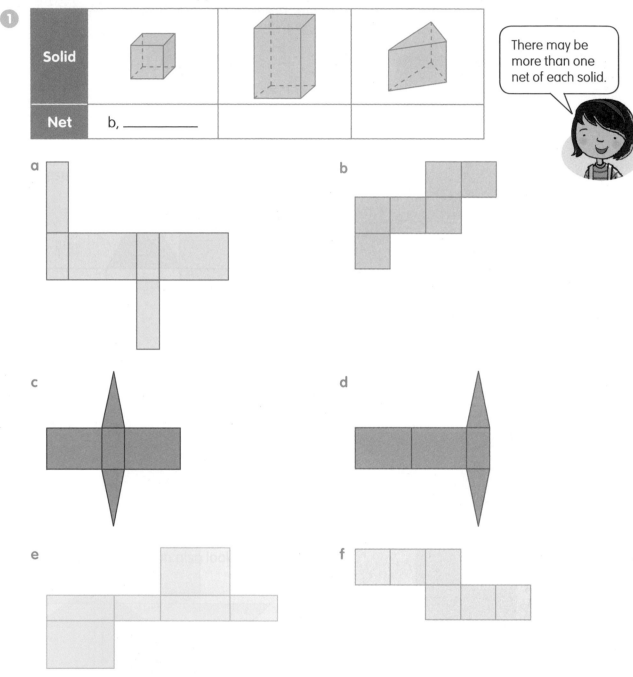		
Net	b, _____		

There may be more than one net of each solid.

a

b

c

d

e

f

Name the solid that each net forms.

2   3   4

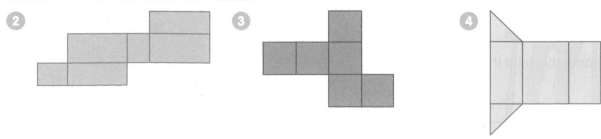

ENGAGE

Make a sketch of each of the following solids given the description of their nets:
The net of solid A has three rectangular faces and two triangular faces.
The net of solid B has one rectangular face and four triangular faces.
Compare your solids to your partner's. Do they look similar? Why or why not?

LEARN Identify the net of a pyramid

1 A pyramid has one base that is a polygon. The other faces are triangles that meet at a common vertex.

The solid shown below is a square pyramid. It has a square face and four faces that are identical isosceles triangles. The square face is the base of the square pyramid.

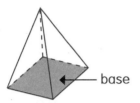

base

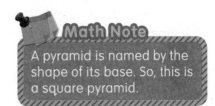

Math Note
A pyramid is named by the shape of its base. So, this is a square pyramid.

These are two nets of the square pyramid.

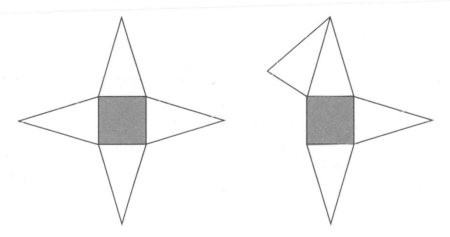

2 The diagram below shows a triangular pyramid and its net.

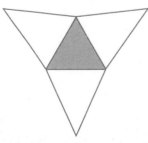

net of triangular pyramid

This triangular pyramid has an equilateral triangle for the base. The other three faces are identical isosceles triangles.

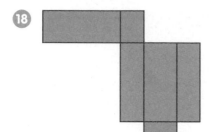

 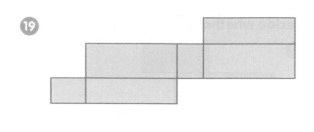

The net of each solid figure is shown below. Write the missing vertices.

20

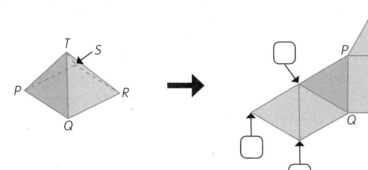

21

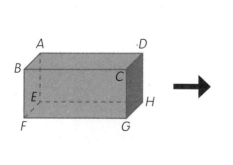

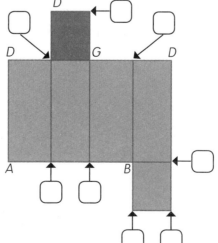

2 Surface Area of Solids

Learning Objective:
• Find the surface area of a prism and a pyramid.

New Vocabulary
surface area

THINK

Two identical cubes are connected to form a rectangular prism. The volume of the rectangular prism is 1,024 cubic centimeters. Find the total area of all the faces of the rectangular prism.

ENGAGE

a Recall how you find the area of a square. How would you find the total area of all of the faces of a cube? Explain to your partner.

b If the side length of each square is increased by 1 unit, find the new total area of all the faces of the cube. Show and explain your thinking.

LEARN Find the ~~surface area~~ of a cube

1 A wooden cubical box is painted green all over.
The total area painted green is the surface area of the box.

2 The wooden cube has edges measuring 5 centimeters each. To find the surface area of the cube, you can draw a net of the cube.

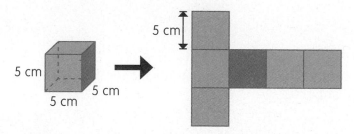

5 cm, 5 cm, 5 cm, 5 cm

The surface area of the cube is equal to the sum of the areas of its six square faces.

Area of one square face = 5 • 5
                        = 25 cm²

Surface area of cube = 6 • 25
                     = 150 cm²

The surface area of a cube is the area of its net.

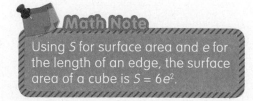
Math Note
Using S for surface area and e for the length of an edge, the surface area of a cube is $S = 6e^2$.

TRY Practice finding the surface area of a cube

Solve.

1 A cube has edges measuring 6 inches each. Find the surface area of the cube.

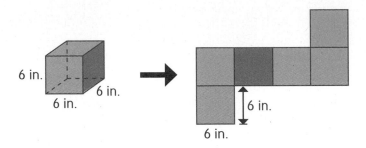

6 in.

6 in.

6 in.

6 in.

6 in.

Area of one square face = _____ • _____

= _____ in²

Surface area of cube = _____ • _____

= _____ in²

ENGAGE

a Recall how you find the area of a rectangle. Then, discuss with your partner how you can find the surface area of a rectangular prism. Are there other ways? How do you know?

b What happens to the new area of the rectangular prism when the length of each edge is doubled? Show and explain your thinking.

LEARN Find the surface area of a rectangular and a triangular prism

1 A rectangular prism measures 12 inches long, 8 inches wide, and 4 inches high. Find the surface area of the rectangular prism.

To find the surface area, draw a net of the rectangular prism.

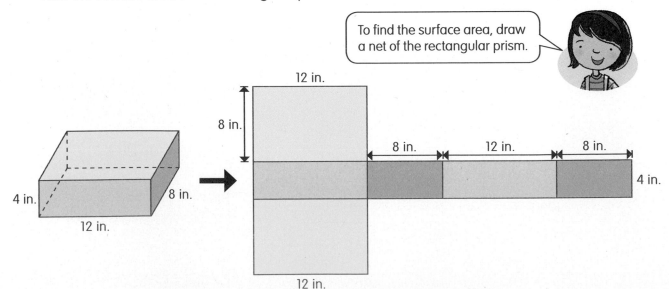

12 in.

8 in.

8 in.   12 in.   8 in.

4 in.

4 in.   8 in.

12 in.

12 in.

© 2020 Marshall Cavendish Education Pte Ltd

The opposite faces of a rectangular prism are identical rectangles.
In the net, each pair of identical faces is of the same color.

The total area of the two **orange** and two **green** faces is
equal to the area of a rectangle of length
12 + 8 + 12 + 8 = 40 inches and width 4 inches.

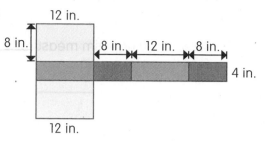

Total area of two **orange** and two **green** faces = 40 · 4
$$= 160 \text{ in}^2$$

Area of two **blue** rectangular bases = 2 · (12 · 8)
$$= 2 · 96$$
$$= 192 \text{ in}^2$$

Surface area of rectangular prism = 160 + 192
$$= 352 \text{ in}^2$$

2 The triangular prism below has three rectangular faces. Its bases are identical
isosceles triangles. Find the surface area of the triangular prism.

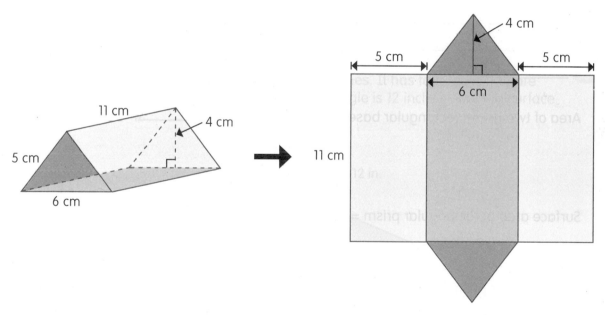

Total area of two **blue** rectangles and one **red** face = (5 + 6 + 5) · 11
$$= 16 · 11$$
$$= 176 \text{ cm}^2$$

Area of two **orange** triangular bases = $2 \cdot \left(\frac{1}{2} \cdot 6 \cdot 4\right)$
$$= 2 · 12$$
$$= 24 \text{ cm}^2$$

Surface area of triangular prism = 176 + 24
$$= 200 \text{ cm}^2$$

The surface area of a prism is the area of its net.

Math Note
The surface area of a prism is
equal to the perimeter of the base
multiplied by the height, and then
added to the sum of the areas of
the two bases.

▶ **Method 2**
Using the formula for finding the volume of a rectangular prism,

length · width · height $= 4\frac{1}{2} \cdot 1 \cdot 1\frac{1}{2}$

$$= \frac{9}{2} \cdot 1 \cdot \frac{3}{2}$$

$$= \frac{27}{4}$$

$$= 6\frac{3}{4} \text{ in}^3$$

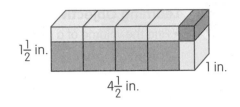

$1\frac{1}{2}$ in.

1 in.

$4\frac{1}{2}$ in.

2 Since **length · width = area of base**,
Volume of a rectangular prism = **length · width** · height
                                = **area of base** · height

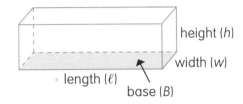

height (h)

width (w)

length (ℓ)

base (B)

The volume of a rectangular prism of length ℓ, width w, and height h is given by
$V = \ell wh$ or $V = Bh$, where B represents the area of the base.

3 A rectangular prism measures 8.4 centimeters by 5.5 centimeters
by 9 centimeters. What is its volume?

$V = \ell wh$
$= 8.4 \cdot 5.5 \cdot 9$
$= 415.8 \text{ cm}^3$

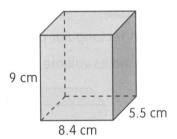

9 cm

5.5 cm

8.4 cm

Math Talk

What if you turn the rectangular prism in **3** on its side
such that a different face is the base? How do you find
the volume? Does the volume change? Explain.

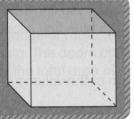

Activity Determining the relationship between volume and surface area of rectangular prisms

Work in pairs.

① Using unit cubes, build the cube and the rectangular prism as shown below.

② Find the volume of the cube and the volume of the rectangular prism. What do you notice about their volumes?

③ Find the surface area of the cube and the surface area of the rectangular prism. What do you notice about their surface areas?

④ Now, build these prisms using unit cubes.

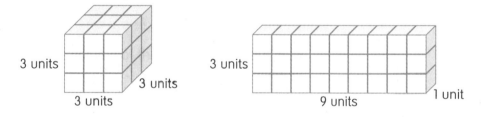

⑤ Find the volume of the cube and the volume of the rectangular prism. What do you notice about their volumes?

⑥ Find the surface area of the cube and the surface area of the rectangular prism. What do you notice about their surface areas?

⑦ **Mathematical Habit 3** Construct viable arguments

Based on your observations, what can you conclude about prisms with the same volume? Which one of the two prisms in ① and ④ has a smaller surface area? Discuss with your partner and explain your thinking.

Solve.

1 A large aquarium is in the shape of a rectangular prism. Find the volume of water needed to fill $\frac{3}{4}$ of the aquarium.

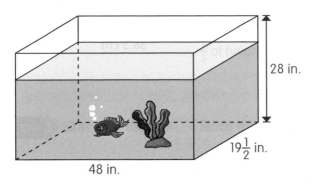

28 in.

$19\frac{1}{2}$ in.

48 in.

Height of water level needed = _____ • _____

= _____ in.

Volume of water needed = _____ • _____ • _____

= _____ in³

To fill $\frac{3}{4}$ of the aquarium, _____ cubic inches of water are needed.

2 A rectangular container has a square base of side 10 centimeters and a height of 30 centimeters. It is filled with 1.2 liters of water. Find the height of the water level.

Volume of water = _____ L

= _____ mL

= _____ cm³

Height of water level = _____ ÷ (_____ • _____)

= _____ ÷ _____

= _____ cm

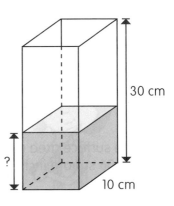

30 cm

?

10 cm

The height of the water level is _____ centimeters.

3 A rectangular tank of length 28 centimeters has two square faces. When completely filled, it can hold 9.072 liters of water. Find the length of each side of a square face.

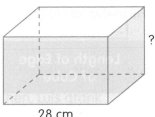

28 cm

Capacity = 9.072 L

Capacity of tank = _____ L

= _____ cm³

Area of square face = _____ ÷ _____

= _____ cm²

Since _____ • _____ = _____, the length of each side of a square face is

_____ centimeters.

4 A storage container is in the shape of a square prism. The container is 15 inches tall and has a volume of 960 cubic inches. Find the surface area of the container.

15 in.

$V = Bh$

_____ = B • _____

_____ ÷ _____ = B • _____ ÷ _____

_____ = B

Since _____ • _____ = _____, the length of each side of a square base is

_____ inches.

Surface area = perimeter of base • height + area of two bases

= (_____ + _____ + _____ + _____) • _____ +

_____ • _____

= _____ • _____ + _____

= _____ + _____

= _____ in²

The surface area of the container is _____ square inches.

Problem Solving with Heuristics

1 The volume of a cube is 1,000 cubic centimeters. If each edge of the cube is tripled in length, what will the volume of the cube be?

2 The volume of a cube is x cubic feet and its surface area is x square feet, where x represents the same number. Find the length of each edge of the cube.

3 Container A was filled with water to the brim. Then, some of the water was poured into empty Container B until the height of the water in both containers became the same. Find the new height of water in both containers.

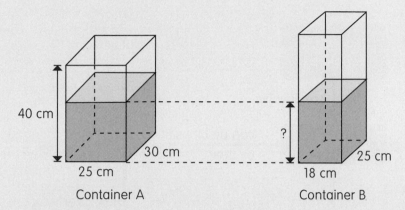

Container A

Container B

CHAPTER WRAP-UP

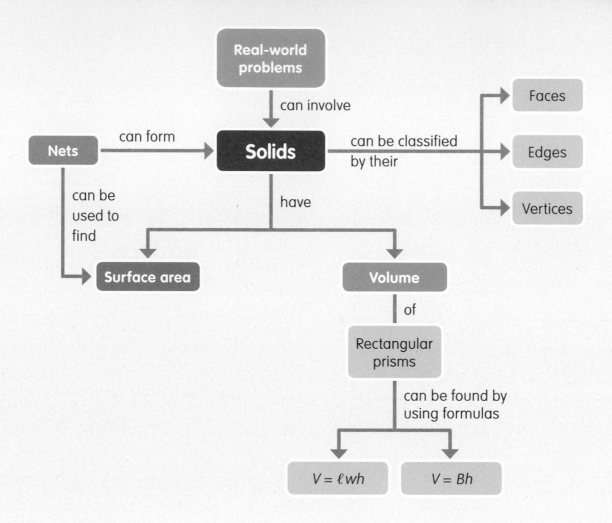

KEY CONCEPTS

• A prism is a solid with two parallel identical bases joined by rectangular faces.

• A pyramid is a solid with a base that can be any polygon. Its other faces are triangles that meet at a common vertex.

• A net can be folded to form a solid. A solid may have more than one net.

• The surface area of a prism or pyramid is the sum of the areas of its faces or the area of its net.

• The volume of a rectangular prism can be found by multiplying its length by its width by its height, or by multiplying its base area and its height.

Match each of the solid figures to its net.

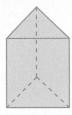 ①

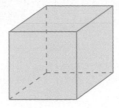 ②

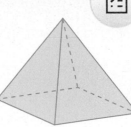 ③

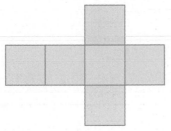 ④

⑤

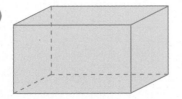
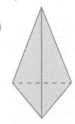
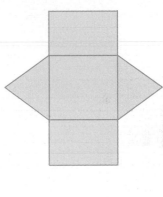

a

b

c

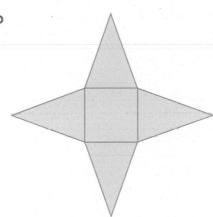

d

e

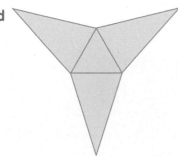

Find the surface area of each solid.

6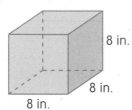

8 in.
8 in.
8 in.

7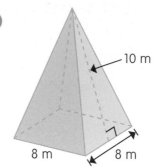

10 m

8 m   8 m

Find the volume of each solid.

8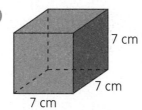

7 cm
7 cm
7 cm

9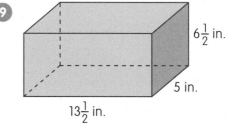

$6\frac{1}{2}$ in.

5 in.

$13\frac{1}{2}$ in.

10 The solid below is made up of cubes, each with edge length of $\frac{1}{2}$ inch.

What is the volume of the solid?

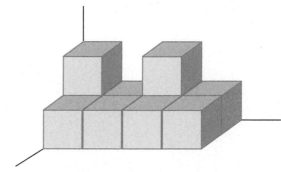

11) A fish tank is 50 centimeters long, 30 centimeters wide, and 40 centimeters high.
It contains water up to a height of 28 centimeters. How many more cubic centimeters
of water are needed to fill the tank to a height of 35 centimeters?

12) The net of a square pyramid is shown below. Given that its base area is
196 square inches and the height of each triangular face is 16 inches,
find the surface area of the square pyramid.

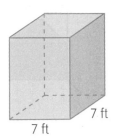

16 in.

base area = 196 in²

13) The volume of a rectangular prism is 441 cubic feet. It has a square base
with edges 7 feet long.

a Find the height of the prism.

7 ft

7 ft

b Find the surface area of the prism.

c Aki then used a piece of plastic to completely wrap the candle. He wrapped it in such a way that no portions of plastic overlapped. Draw the piece of plastic he used.

d What was the total surface area of the candle?

2 Jennifer used a rectangular box measuring $2\frac{1}{2}$ feet by $1\frac{1}{2}$ feet by 2 feet to store the candles she made.

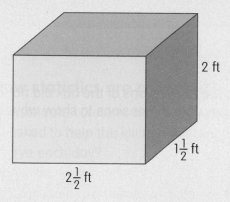

2 ft

$1\frac{1}{2}$ ft

$2\frac{1}{2}$ ft

a What was the volume of the box?

b Jennifer made some large cubical candles of edge length $\frac{1}{2}$ foot. How many of such candles could she fit into the box?

c Jennifer also made some smaller cubical candles of edge length $\frac{1}{4}$ foot. How many of such candles could she fit into the box? How can you use the answer from b to find the answer?

TRY Practice collecting and tabulating data to answer a statistical question

Decide if each sentence is a statistical question. Answer Yes or No.

1 How many books did you read last month?

2 How many books did your classmates read last month?

3 What is the average temperature in April?

4 How many days are there this year?

Answer each question.

5 Irene used a questionnaire to find out the number of brothers or sisters her classmates have. Then, she used a tally chart to record her results.

a Fill in the tally chart.

Number of Brothers or Sisters of Irene's Classmates

Number of Brothers or Sisters	Tally	Frequency
0	III	
1	HHT IIII	
2	HHT II	
3	HHT	
4	II	
5 or more	I	

b How many siblings do most of Irene's classmates have?

c How many of Irene's classmates have 2 or more brothers or sisters?

d How many classmates does Irene have altogether?

INDEPENDENT PRACTICE

Decide if each sentence is a statistical question. Answer Yes or No.

1 What is your favorite color?

2 What is the most liked color among your classmates?

3 How tall is the giraffe?

4 What are the heights of the trees in a garden?

5 How many hours do the sixth-graders volunteer in a year?

6 What is the difference between the number of days in March and April?

Answer each question.

7 A shampoo company wanted to find out more about its customers. The company conducted a survey to find out the income bracket of some of its customers. A tally chart is used to record the findings as shown.

a Fill in the tally chart.

Weekly Income of Customers

Weekly Income	Tally	Frequency
Below $500	ⵗ⵫ ||	
$500–$1,000	ⵗ⵫ ⵗ⵫ ⵗ⵫ ||||	
Over $1,000	||||	

b How many customers have a weekly income of $1,000 or less?

c How many customers took part in the survey?

8 Axel conducted a survey to find out the favorite fruit of some sixth graders. The students were asked to choose a fruit from the following list: apple, orange, strawberry, grapes, and peach. These are the data Axel collected:

strawberry	peach	apple	apple
orange	strawberry	strawberry	grapes
strawberry	apple	strawberry	apple
peach	orange	grapes	orange
strawberry	apple	strawberry	grapes

Fill in the tally chart.

Favorite Fruit of Sixth Graders

Fruit	Tally	Frequency
Apple		
Orange		
Strawberry		
Grapes		
Peach		

9 A teacher wanted to find out the duration (in hours, h) per week his students spent on math homework. The duration (in hours, h) reported by each student is listed below:

5, 3, 6, 8, 2, 4, 2, 1, 9, 1, 9, 6, 4, 6, 5, 1, 10, 1, 5, 6, 7, 8, 6, 10, 7, 5, 2, 8

a Arrange the duration in ascending order.

b Fill in the tally chart.

Amount of Time Spent on Math Homework Per Week

Duration (h)	Tally	Frequency
0–3		
4–7		
8–10		

c How many students were surveyed?

d How many students spent more than 3 hours per week on their math homework?

Name: _____ Date: _____

2 Dot Plots

Learning Objectives:
- Display and analyze data using a dot plot.
- Find the range of a data set.

New Vocabulary
dot plot
range
symmetrical
skewed

THINK

Use an example to compare frequency tables and dot plots as methods of displaying a data set. For each method, describe how the data set is displayed and state its advantages.

ENGAGE

Sean conducted a survey to find out the shoe sizes of some classmates. Their shoe sizes are as follows.

8	7	10	8	7
9	8	7	8	9

Consider various ways to organize and represent the data using a table and a graph. Share your ideas.

LEARN Use a ~~dot plot~~ to represent numerical data

1 The number of text messages sent by some students in a day is as follows.

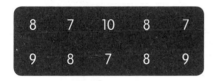

12	11	10	15	13
15	12	11	12	11

TRY Practice interpreting data from a dot plot

Describe the data.

1. The number of movies some students had watched last month is shown in the dot plot.

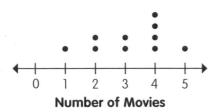

Number of Movies

a The _____ dots represent _____ students.

b The data values are from _____ to _____.

The range is _____ – _____ = _____.

c Most of the data values are from _____ to _____.

d The dot plot has a "tail" on the _____. The distribution is skewed to the _____.

e Most of the students had watched about _____ to _____ movies, and all of

them had watched _____ to _____ movies.

2. The number of points 12 players scored in a volleyball game is shown in the dot plot. Briefly describe the number of points scored by the players.

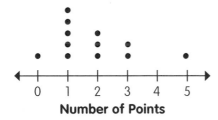

Number of Points

© 2020 Marshall Cavendish Education Pte Ltd

INDEPENDENT PRACTICE

Draw a dot plot for each set of data.

1 The years of service of 18 employees in a company are shown below.

7	8	4	3	10	3
2	10	7	6	8	2
1	4	11	12	6	9

2 A group of 24 students was asked the number of states that they have visited. The results are recorded in the table.

Number of States Visited	0	1	2	3	4	5	6	7
Frequency	2	4	5	2	2	6	2	1

2 The data show the distances (in centimeters, cm) 40 students achieved in a standing long jump session.

171	111	185	161	200	175	153	191	168	173
211	170	173	141	170	188	150	171	175	168
163	175	203	189	170	163	179	167	184	160
172	243	174	165	177	159	199	205	172	129

a Group the data into suitable intervals and tabulate them.
Explain your choice of intervals.

b Draw a histogram using the interval.

ENGAGE

Ivan drew the histogram on the right.
What information is missing?
What do you think the data represents?
Correct Ivan's graph. Share your ideas.

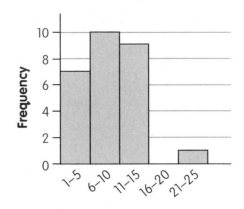

LEARN Interpret data from a histogram

1 The histogram shows the number of representatives from each state in the U.S. Congress in 2018. Briefly describe the data.

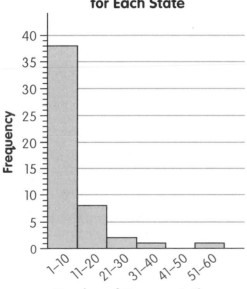

Congressional Representatives for Each State

There are 50 states in the United States.

Most of the states sent 1 to 10 representatives to the U.S. Congress in 2018.

The histogram has a "tail" to the right. Most of the data values are to the right of the most frequent value, so the shape of the histogram is right-skewed.

No states sent 41 to 50 representatives.

Only one state sent 51 to 60 representatives, which is an outlier in the data.

© 2020 Marshall Cavendish Education Pte Ltd

6 The wait times (in minutes, min) of 60 customers at a service center are given below.
Two customers waited for at least 30 minutes.

Wait Time (min)	2–5	6–9	10–13	14–17	18–21	22–25	26–29	30–33	34–37
Frequency	x	8	22	16	4	3	3	y	1

a Find the values of x and y.

b What fraction of the customers waited for less than 10 minutes?

c Draw a histogram using the given intervals to represent the data.
Briefly describe the data.

d Draw a histogram for the above data using these intervals: 2 to 13, 14 to 25, and 26 to 37.

e **Mathematical Habit 2 Use mathematical reasoning**
Compare the two histograms. When would each one be more useful?

1 **Mathematical Habit** **2** **Use mathematical reasoning**

Eric recorded the number of hours that a group of students volunteered in a year. He drew the dot plot below to display the results.

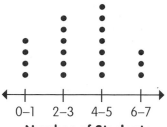

Number of Students

Eric's dot plot was not drawn correctly. Explain the mistakes he made.

2 **Mathematical Habit** **2** **Use mathematical reasoning**

Layla collected data on the duration (in minutes, min) 20 visitors spent at a store in a day.

15	18	27	15	24	22	30	16	21	15
20	25	25	14	15	20	23	5	15	10

Layla wants to draw a histogram to represent the data. Explain the steps and guide her to draw the histogram.

5 The data show the distances a golfer hit (in yards, yd) in a long drive championship.

244	252	267	245	257	270	250	261	251	274
263	248	256	273	270	248	265	271	260	278
254	250	255	252	249	263	273	268	256	269

a Group the data into suitable intervals and tabulate them. Explain your choice of interval.

b Draw a histogram using the interval. Briefly describe the data.

© 2020 Marshall Cavendish Education Pte Ltd

6 The table shows the number of cars that passed a traffic light during peak hours on a Friday morning.

Time (A.M.)	7:00–7:29	7:30–7:59	8:00–8:29	8:30–8:59	9:00–9:29	9:30–9:59
Frequency	22	45	64	57	27	25

a How many cars were observed altogether?

b Draw a histogram to represent the data.

c Describe the distribution of the data. Explain the shape of the histogram.

1 Group the data into suitable intervals and tabulate them. Explain your choice of intervals.

2 Draw a histogram to represent the data using the intervals you chose.

3 Write two statistical questions that can be answered by the histogram and answer them.

4 Write an example of a question that refers to the data but that is not statistical.

How do shoemakers know what customers will buy?

The quantity of shoes manufactured for each size depends on what retailers have ordered. Production can be tailored to meet the demand. This can be done by finding a value around which most orders cluster. It helps to reduce waste in the manufacturing process.

In statistics, measures of central tendency and spread are used to summarize large amounts of data. Learning how to summarize data is an important part of any business. In this chapter, you will learn to summarize and make meaningful interpretation of data.

How can you summarize and interpret data to solve real-world problems?

TRY **Practice finding the mean of a data set using a dot plot**

Solve. Use the data in the dot plot.

1 A group of volunteers sold coupons to raise money for a food pantry. The dot plot on the right shows the number of coupons sold by each volunteer. Each dot represents one volunteer.

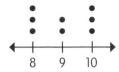

Number of Coupons

What was the mean number of coupons sold by the group of volunteers?

_____ volunteers sold 8 coupons each.

→ _____ × _____ = _____ coupons sold

_____ volunteers sold 9 coupons each.

→ _____ × _____ = _____ coupons sold

_____ volunteers sold 10 coupons each.

→ _____ × _____ = _____ coupons sold

Mean number of coupons = $\dfrac{\text{Total number of coupons sold}}{\text{Number of volunteers}}$

$= \dfrac{\boxed{} + \boxed{} + \boxed{}}{\boxed{}}$

= _____

The mean number of coupons sold by the group of volunteers was _____.

ENGAGE

The mean of four numbers is 32. The mean of two of the numbers is 28. Discuss the steps you would follow to find the mean of the other two numbers.

LEARN Find the total and a missing number from the mean

1. Sophie recorded the widths of 6 books and found the mean to be 21.2 centimeters. She lost one of the books. The widths of the remaining five books are 12.3 centimeters, 16.5 centimeters, 18.8 centimeters, 22.4 centimeters, and 26.0 centimeters. Find the width of the missing book.

Total width of 6 books = Mean × Number of books
$$= 21.2 \times 6$$
$$= 127.2 \text{ cm}$$

> To find the total of a set of items, multiply the mean by the number of items.

Total width of remaining five books = 12.3 + 16.5 + 18.8 + 22.4 + 26.0
$$= 96 \text{ cm}$$

$$127.2 - 96 = 31.2$$

The width of the missing book is 31.2 centimeters.

Activity Finding mean and using mean to solve problems

Work in groups.

1. Use a centimeter ruler to measure the length of each group member's hand to the nearest tenth of a centimeter. Record your answers in the table below.

Hand Size of Group Members

Name	Hand Length (cm)

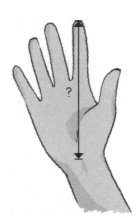

2. Use your data to answer each of the following questions.

   a What is the longest hand length?

   b What is the shortest hand length?

6 The masses of 6 boxes are 34.5 kilograms, 42.6 kilograms, 39.8 kilograms, 40.1 kilograms, 53.4 kilograms, and 33.8 kilograms. Find their mean mass.

7 The table shows a sprinter's times, in seconds, for the 100-meter dash at the first five meets of a season.

Times for 100-meter Dash by Sprinter

Meet Number	1	2	3	4	5
Time (s)	10.09	10.14	10.29	10.07	9.99

What was the sprinter's mean time for the 100-meter dash at these meets?

8 8 ice hockey teams competed in the quarterfinals of a national championship. The dot plot shows the number of goals scored by each team. Each dot represents one team.

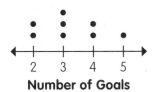

Number of Goals

a What was the total number of goals scored by the 8 teams?

b What was the mean number of goals scored by those teams?

9 The mean of five numbers, 3, 7, 9, 12, and x, is 8. Find the value of x.

10 The mean of a set of 5 numbers is 4.8. Given that the sixth number is x, and the mean of these 6 numbers is 5.5, find the value of x.

11 The mean time for 3 runners was 12.4 seconds, and the mean time for another 6 runners was 11.5 seconds. Calculate the mean time for all the 9 runners.

12 The mean weight of 9 apples is 7.5 ounces. 3 of the apples have a mean weight of 8 ounces. Find the mean weight of the other 6 apples.

13 The mean of 6 numbers is 45. Four of the numbers are 40, 38, 46, and 51. If the remaining two numbers are in the ratio 2 : 3, find the two numbers.

14 A data set consists of 3 numbers, a, b, and c. Write an algebraic expression, in terms of a, b, and c, to represent the mean of the new set of numbers obtained by

a adding 5 to every number in the set.

b doubling every number in the set.

c halving every number in the set.

15 Mathematical Habit 1 Persevere in solving problems
In a series of six class quizzes, Timothy's first four quiz scores are 3, 5, 6, and 8. The mean score of the six quizzes is 6. If the greater of the missing quiz scores is doubled, the mean score becomes $7\frac{1}{3}$. What are the two missing quiz scores?

Timothy's Test Scores

Test	First	Second	Third	Fourth	Fifth	Sixth
Score	3	5	6	8	?	?

16 Mathematical Habit 8 Look for patterns
Find five different numbers whose mean is 12. Explain your strategy.

Name: _____ Date: _____

2 Median

Learning Objectives:
• Find the median of a data set.
• Use the median of a data set to solve problems.

New Vocabulary
median

THINK

The table shows the number of times different number cards were drawn in a game.

Number of Times that Cards were Drawn

Number on Card	Frequency
2	3
4	5
6	8
8	6
10	2

a What is the median of the set of data?
b Show how you can change some numbers in the table so that the median becomes 8.

ENGAGE

Arrange 7, 9, and 6 from least to greatest. Then, identify the value in the middle. How do you find the value in the middle for the numbers, 7, 9, 6, and 4? Share your idea.

LEARN Find the ▓▓▓▓▓ of a data set

1 The median of a data set is another measure of central tendency. The median is the middle value of the set of data.

There are two ways of finding median, depending on whether the data set has an odd or an even number of values.

2. Julia drew three number cards from a box. She wanted to find the middle value, or median, of these numbers.

First, she arranged the numbers from least to greatest.

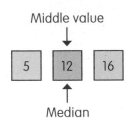

When a data set has an **odd** number of values, identify the middle value, or median, by inspection. The number of values less than the median equals the number of values greater than the median.

Then, she identified the middle value, 12.
So, the median of the three numbers is 12.

3. Jessica then picked another number, 19, from the box. She arranged these numbers in order again.

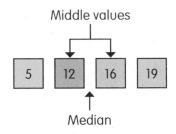

When a data set has an **even** number of values, identify the two middle values. The median is the mean of these two middle values.

Mean of the two middle values $= \dfrac{12 + 16}{2}$

$= \dfrac{28}{2}$

$= 14$

Caution

Remember, the data must be in order before you look for the middle value or values. The data can be arranged from least to greatest, or greatest to least.

So, the median of the four numbers is 14.

Activity Finding the median of a data set

Work in pairs.

1. Shuffle a set of number cards (from 1 to 20) and place them face down. Then, draw five cards randomly from the pile.

2. Arrange the cards you have drawn from least to greatest. Then, find the median of the set of numbers.

3. Repeat the activity by drawing six number cards.

④ Repeat the activity by drawing seven number cards.

⑤ What do you notice about the median in each set of five, six, and seven numbers? Can you say that the more numbers there are in a set, the greater the median? Explain your answer.

TRY Practice finding the median of a data set

Find the median of each data set.

① The data set shows the volumes of water in some containers.

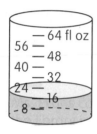 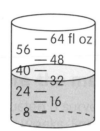 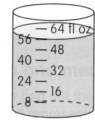 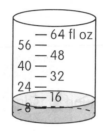

The median volume of water is _____ fluid ounces.

② The data set shows the ages of a group of people.

23 yr, 36 yr, 28 yr, 43 yr, 34 yr, 29 yr

The two middle values are _____ years and _____ years.

Mean of the two middle values = $\dfrac{\boxed{} + \boxed{}}{2}$ = _____ yr

The median age is _____ years.

③ The data set shows the distances some students ran.

$\frac{1}{2}$ mi, $\frac{7}{8}$ mi, $\frac{3}{4}$ mi, $\frac{5}{8}$ mi

The median distance was _____ mile.

12 The median of a set of three unknown numbers is 5. If 3 is added to the least number in the set, give an example of the original set in which

  a the median of the new set of numbers will not be equal to 5.

  b the median of the new set of numbers will still be equal to 5.

13 The median of a set of three unknown numbers is 5. If 2 is subtracted from the greatest number in the set, give an example of the original set in which

  a the median of the new set of numbers will not be equal to 5.

  b the median of the new set of numbers will still be equal to 5.

Name: _____ Date: _____

Mode

Learning Objectives:
- Find the mode of a data set.
- Use the mode of a data set to solve problems.

New Vocabulary
mode
categorical

 THINK

Suppose you spin a number wheel with the numbers 1 to 5. Fill in the table so that the median and the mode of the data set are of the same value.

Numbers Spun on a Number Wheel

Number Spun	1	2	3	4	5
Frequency					

ENGAGE

Toss a number cube 12 times and record the results in the table.

Numbers Tossed on a Number Cube

Number Tossed	1	2	3	4	5	6
Frequency						

Which number is tossed most frequently?

LEARN Find the _____ of a data set

1. The mode of a data set is the value or item that appears most frequently in a set of data. It is the third measure of central tendency.

2. Michael tossed a number cube several times. He recorded the results in the table below.

Number Tossed on a Number Cube

Number Tossed	1	2	3	4	5	6
Frequency	1	2	2	1	3	2

Notice that the number 5 was tossed the most frequently. So, the number 5 is the mode of the set of data.

You can draw a dot plot to show that the number 5 is the mode of the set of data. Each dot represents one toss.

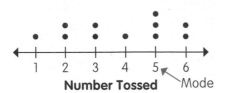

Number Tossed — Mode

The dot plot shows clearly that the number 5 appears the most frequently. So, the number 5 is the mode of the set of data.

TRY Practice finding the mode of a data set

Solve.

1. Justin recorded the 100-meter race times, in seconds, of ten runners on a track team. The data set shows the times that he recorded.

    9.8 s, 9.9 s, 10.0 s, 9.9 s, 10.2 s, 10.1 s, 9.8 s, 10.3 s, 9.9 s, 10.1 s

    a Fill in the table.

    Times of Ten Runners

Time (s)	9.8		10.0			
Frequency	2					

    b Find the mode of this data set.

2. The dot plot shows Emma's scores for ten frames of a bowling game. Each dot represents her scores for one frame.

    Score Per Frame

    a In how many games did Emma score 11 points?

    b What are the modes of this data set?

When a data set has two modes, you can say that the data set is bimodal.

ENGAGE

Write the names of five of your classmates on paper. From the list of names, draw a table to show the frequency of each letter that appears. Which letter appears the most frequently? What is the mode?

LEARN Use mode to summarize a ~~categorical~~ data set

1 A farmer was placing chickens, ducks, and geese in a feeding pen. He recorded the type of birds as C, D, or G as they went into the pen. These are the data he recorded.

D	C	C	C	C	G	D	C	C	C
D	C	D	D	C	C	C	G	D	D
G	C	C	D	C	C	G	D	D	G

This data set is not numeric, so you cannot find the mean or median. However, you can find the mode of the data. Since C appears the most frequently, the mode is chickens.

You can use a bar graph to show the mode.

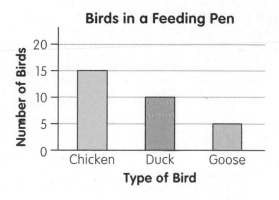

Birds in a Feeding Pen

Notice that the bar representing the number of chickens has the greatest height. So, the number of chickens is the greatest and the mode is chickens.

TRY Practice using mode to summarize a categorical data set

Find the mode of each set of data.

1 There are 9 teachers, 79 boys, and 65 girls at a school camp.

2 There are 1 laundry shop, 14 garment shops, 3 photographic shops, 5 shoe shops, and 9 food stores in a mall.

3 The data set shows the weights of some students' school bags.

5.5 kg, 6.6 kg, 4.8 kg, 4.3 kg, 5.5 kg, 4.3 kg, 5.5 kg, 6.6 kg, 4.5 kg, 5.5 kg

Activity Comparing mean, median, and mode

Work in pairs.

1 Cut out, fold, and tape the net of a rectangular prism (with pairs of opposite faces numbered 10, 11, or 12) provided by your teacher.

2 Take turns to toss the rectangular prism 40 times and record the number tossed each time.

3 Record your results in the table below.

Numbers Tossed on a Rectangular Prism

Number Tossed	Tally	Frequency
10		
11		
12		

4 From the set of data collected, find the

a mean.   **b** median.   **c** mode.

5 **a** Find the area of each face to the nearest tenth of a square centimeter.
Find the ratio of the total area of faces numbered 10 to the total area of faces numbered 11 to the total area of faces numbered 12.

b Find the ratio of the number of times the number 10 is tossed to the number of times the number 11 is tossed to the number of times the number 12 is tossed.

c Compare the two ratios. Why do you think you get this result?

6 Compare your findings with your classmates'. What do you notice?

INDEPENDENT PRACTICE

Find the mode or modes of each data set.

1. 5, 6, 4, 5, 8, 9, 9, 3, 4, 5

2. 13, 31, 12, 45, 6, 19, 21, 12, 31

3. 8.5, 6.5, 7.8, 6.5. 6.4, 2.3, 4.5, 5.4, 7.8, 5.5, 7.8

Find the mode.

4. The scores of a basketball team in a series of games are 76, 85, 65, 58, 68, 72, 91, and 68. Find the mode.

5. The table shows sizes of shoes and the number of pairs of shoes sold at a shop last month.

Number of Pairs of Shoes Sold Last Month

Size	6.5	7	7.5	8	8.5	9	9.5	10	10.5
Number of Pairs	5	15	21	30	30	31	13	8	3

Find the mode.

6. Tickets for a concert are priced at $20, $30, $40, $50, or $100. The table shows the number of tickets sold at each price.

Number of Tickets Sold at Each Price

Price ($)	20	30	40	50	100
Number of Tickets	40	55	95	84	48

Find the mode.

Solve.

7. The data set shows the number of goals scored by a soccer team in 17 matches.

3, 2, 1, 0, 2, 4, 1, 0, 2, 3, 4, 2, 3, 2, 1, 2, 5

a Draw a dot plot to represent the data.

The median of a data set divides the data into two equal parts, the lower half, and the upper half. The data below the median lie in the lower half and the data above the median lie in the upper half.

Next, find the median of the lower half and the median of the upper half.
The median of the lower half is the first quartile or lower quartile, Q_1.
The median of the data set is the second quartile, Q_2.
The median of the upper half is the third quartile or upper quartile, Q_3.

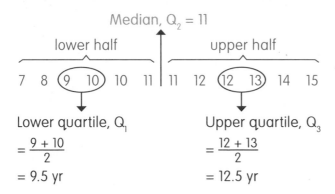

Lower quartile, Q_1
$$= \frac{9 + 10}{2}$$
$$= 9.5 \text{ yr}$$

Upper quartile, Q_3
$$= \frac{12 + 13}{2}$$
$$= 12.5 \text{ yr}$$

The lower quartile is 9.5 years and the upper quartile is 12.5 years.

2 Besides using measures of central tendency to summarize a data set, we can also use measures of variability to find the spread of the data. The simplest measure of variability is the range.

Referring to the data set in **1**,
Range = Greatest value – Least value
$$= 15 - 7$$
$$= 8 \text{ yr}$$

The range is 8 years.

Another way to measure variability is to find the interquartile range. It is the difference between the lower and upper quartiles.

Referring to the data set in **1**,
Interquartile range = $Q_3 - Q_1$
$$= 12.5 - 9.5$$
$$= 3 \text{ yr}$$

The interquartile range is 3 years.

Math Talk

Explain what the interquartile range means. Compare the range and the interquartile range of the data set in **1**. Discuss the differences between the two measures.

3 You can summarize the quartiles and interquartile range of the data set in a diagram:

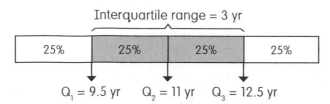

Interquartile range = 3 yr

| 25% | 25% | 25% | 25% |

$Q_1 = 9.5$ yr $Q_2 = 11$ yr $Q_3 = 12.5$ yr

Since the quartiles divide the data into four equal parts, each part represents 25% of the data.

From the diagram, you can see that:
• 25% of the students' ages are 9.5 years or less.
• 50% of the students' ages are 11 years or less.
• 75% of the students' ages are 12.5 years or less.

Notice that the ages of 50% of the students are between 9.5 years and 12.5 years.

From the diagram, you can also interpret that:
• 75% of the students' ages are 9.5 years or more.
• 50% of the students' ages are 11 years or more.
• 25% of the students' ages are 12.5 years or more.

TRY Practice finding the quartiles and interquartile range of a data set

Solve.

1 The heights, in meters, of 12 students are listed below in ascending order.

a Find the median, the lower quartile, and the upper quartile of the data set.

1.4   1.5   1.5 | 1.6   1.6   1.7 | 1.7   1.7   1.8 | 1.8   1.9   1.9

Lower quartile, Q_1 Median, Q_2 Upper quartile, Q_3

= _____ m   = _____ m   = _____ m

b Find the interquartile range.

Interquartile range = $Q_3 - Q_1$

$$= \underline{\qquad} - \underline{\qquad}$$

$$= \underline{\qquad} \text{ m}$$

c Complete each statement.

25% of the students' heights are _____ meters or less.

50% of the students' heights are _____ meters or less.

75% of the students' heights are _____ meters or less.

A box plot is constructed on a number line using five values:
- the least value,
- the lower quartile, Q_1,
- the median, Q_2,
- the upper quartile, Q_3, and
- the greatest value.

These five values are known as a 5-point summary.

The box plot for the given data set is shown below.

Least value	30
Lower quartile, Q_1	35
Median, Q_2	45
Upper quartile, Q_3	60
Greatest value	80

Unlike a dot plot, a box plot does not show individual data values. It summarizes a data set using five values and is useful for large data sets.

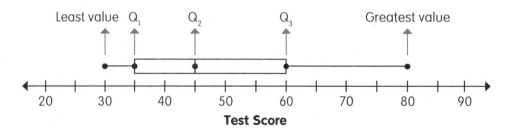

From the box plot, you can see that:
- the box contains the middle 50% of the data.
- the length of the box represents the interquartile range.
- the two horizontal lines contain the remaining 50% of the data that are not within the middle 50%.

Math Talk

How do you describe the distribution of the test scores using the box plot? Include descriptions of a measure of center and a measure of variability. Discuss.

© 2020 Marshall Cavendish Education Pte Ltd

Solve.

1. The box plot summarizes the lifespans, in years, of rhinoceroses in a nature preserve. State the least value, the greatest value, the median, the lower quartile, and the upper quartile. Then, find the interquartile range.

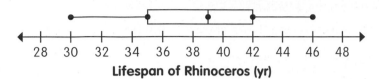

Lifespan of Rhinoceros (yr)

a Least value = _____ yr   b Greatest value = _____ yr

c Median = _____ yr   d Lower quartile = _____ yr

e Upper quartile = _____ yr   f Interquartile range = _____ yr

2. The table shows the number of cars sold by ten companies on a certain day.

Number of Cars Sold in Ten Companies

Company	A	B	C	D	E	F	G	H	I	J
Number of Cars	25	30	20	15	18	15	12	12	10	8

a Arrange the number of cars in ascending order.

b Find the least number, the greatest number, the median, the lower quartile, and the upper quartile of the data.

c Draw a box plot of the number of cars sold by the ten companies.

Math Talk

How do you describe the distribution of the number of cars sold using the box plot? Include descriptions of a measure of center and a measure of variability. Discuss.

TRY Practice calculating the mean absolute deviation of a data set

Solve.

1. The speeds of ten cars, in miles per hour, on a highway are recorded below.

| 55 | 52 | 57 | 54 | 51 | 53 | 45 | 57 |

a Find the mean speed.

Mean speed

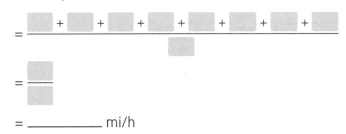

= _____ mi/h

The mean speed is _____ miles per hour.

b Fill in the table.

Speed of Car (mi/h)	Mean (mi/h)	Deviation from the Mean (mi/h)

Find the deviation between each data value and the mean by subtracting the lesser value from the greater value. The distance from the mean is never a negative value.

c Calculate the mean absolute deviation.

Mean absolute deviation

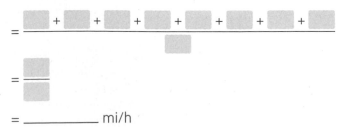

= _____ mi/h

The mean absolute deviation is _____ miles per hour.

INDEPENDENT PRACTICE

For each box plot, state the least value, the greatest value, the median, the lower quartile, and the upper quartile. Then, find the interquartile range.

1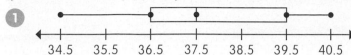

34.5   35.5   36.5   37.5   38.5   39.5   40.5

2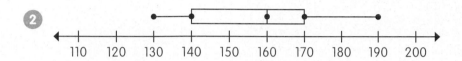

110   120   130   140   150   160   170   180   190   200

3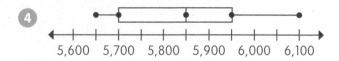

10   12   14   16   18   20   22   24   26   28

4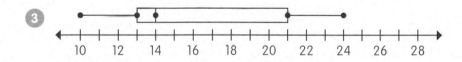

5,600   5,700   5,800   5,900   6,000   6,100

Draw a box plot for each set of five values.

5 Lower quartile = 34, median = 37, upper quartile = 40, least value = 30, greatest value = 45

6 Lower quartile = 114, median = 118, upper quartile = 123, least value = 110, greatest value = 128

7 Lower quartile = 3,320, median = 3,360, upper quartile = 3,380, least value = 3,000, greatest value = 3,400

8 Lower quartile = 96.1, median = 96.6, upper quartile = 97.0, least value = 95.7, greatest value = 97.4

Calculate the mean absolute deviation for each data set. Round your answer to the nearest hundredth, where necessary.

9 758, 762, 745, 739, 740, 760, 767

10 52, 52, 55, 53, 59, 56, 60, 54, 57, 55

11 13.4, 10.5, 10.0, 13.6, 14.5, 16.9, 11.7, 10.2

12 21.15, 21.16, 21.25, 21.22, 21.36, 21.38, 21.49, 21.22, 21.11

Solve.

13 The prices, in cents, of 12 apples are shown below.

| 58 | 51 | 63 | 45 | 57 | 57 | 62 | 62 | 49 | 43 | 41 | 60 |

a Calculate the lower quartile, the median, and the upper quartile.

b Draw a box plot of the prices of the apples.

c Calculate the mean price of the apples.

d Calculate the mean absolute deviation of the prices of the apples. Round your answer to the nearest hundredth.

14 The heights, in centimeters, of ten plants are shown below.

| 18.2 | 23.8 | 26.2 | 16.6 | 19.6 | 20.8 | 17.9 | 18.9 | 23.0 | 20.0 |

a Calculate the three quartiles.

b Draw a box plot of the heights of the plants.

c Calculate the mean height.

d Calculate the mean absolute deviation of the heights.

e **Mathematical Habit 2** **Use mathematical reasoning**
What can you tell about the heights of the ten plants? Use your answers from **a** to **d** to help you explain.

© 2020 Marshall Cavendish Education Pte Ltd

Real-World Problems: Measures of Central Tendency and Variability

Learning Objective:
• Solve real-world problems involving measures of central tendency and variability.

 **THINK**

The table below shows the number of cars in 15 homes.

Number of Homes with Cars

Number of Cars	0	1	2	3	4
Number of Homes	2	x	4	3	y

Given that the median = mode = 2, find the values of x and y.
Then, calculate the mean absolute deviation. What can you infer about the variability of the data set?

ENGAGE

The table shows the coins Natalie has.

Number of Coins of Different Values

Value of Coin	1¢	5¢	10¢	25¢
Number of Coins	1	3	8	2

Find the mean, median, and mode of the data set. Consider each measure of central tendency. Which is best to describe the amount of money Natalie has? Which is best to describe the type of coins Natalie has? Discuss.

LEARN Decide whether to use mean, median, or mode to solve real-world problems

1 The table shows the sizes of in-line skates and the number of pairs of skates sold in a month.

Number of Pairs of In-Line Skates Sold

Size	Number of Pairs
6	12
7	15
8	18
9	9
10	6

a What is the mean size of the in-line skates sold?
b What is the median size of the in-line skates sold?
c What is the modal size of the in-line skates sold?
d Which measure of central tendency best describes the data set?

What does the table show? What are the different measures of central tendency? What do I need to find?

STEP 1 Understand the problem.

TRY Practice using box plots to compare two data sets to solve real-world problems

Solve.

1 The time taken, in minutes, by students from two schools to travel from home to school are summarized in the box plots.

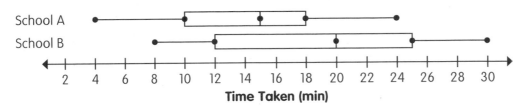

Time Taken (min)

a Compare the medians of the two schools.

Median time taken by students of School A = _____ min

Median time taken by students of School B = _____ min

The median time taken by students of School A is _____ that of School B.

b Compare the interquartile ranges of the two schools.

Interquartile range of School A = 18 – 10

= _____ min

Interquartile range of School B = 25 – 12

= _____ min

The interquartile range of School A is _____ that of School B.

c Relate the interquartile ranges to the distributions. Which school has a less variability in the time taken by students to travel from home to school? Explain.

© 2020 Marshall Cavendish Education Pte Ltd

ENGAGE

Create a spinner with a paperclip and a pencil.

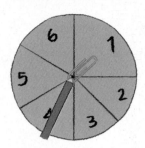

Spin the spinner ten times and record your results in the table.

Number Spun on a Spinner

Number Spun	1	2	3	4	5	6
Frequency						

Find the mean and mean absolute deviation. Compare your answers with your partner's. What can you infer about the variability of the two data sets?

LEARN Use means and mean absolute deviations to compare two data sets to solve real-world problems

1. The table shows the weights, in pounds, of barley two grocers, A and B, sold in the morning over a certain week.

Weights (lb) of Barley Sold

Day	Sun.	Mon.	Tue.	Wed.	Thu.	Fri.	Sat.
Grocer A	9	8	10	10	8	8	10
Grocer B	15	2	5	8	11	9	13

 a Find the mean weight, in pounds, of barley each grocer sold.

$$\text{Mean weight of barley Grocer A sold} = \frac{9 + 8 + 10 + 10 + 8 + 8 + 10}{7}$$

$$= \frac{63}{7}$$

$$= 9 \text{ lb}$$

The mean weight of barley Grocer A sold was 9 pounds.

$$\text{Mean weight of barley Grocer B sold} = \frac{15 + 2 + 5 + 8 + 11 + 9 + 13}{7}$$

$$= \frac{63}{7}$$

$$= 9 \text{ lb}$$

The mean weight of barley Grocer B sold was 9 pounds.

b Calculate the mean absolute deviation of the weights, in pounds, of barley each grocer sold. Round your answers to the nearest whole number.

Weight (lb) of Barley Grocer A Sold	Mean (lb)	Deviation from the Mean (lb)
9	9	0
8	9	1
10	9	1
10	9	1
8	9	1
8	9	1
10	9	1

Mean absolute deviation of the weights of barley Grocer A sold

$$= \frac{0 + 1 + 1 + 1 + 1 + 1 + 1}{7}$$

$$= \frac{6}{7}$$

= 1 lb (to the nearest whole number)

Weight (lb) of Barley Grocer B Sold	Mean (lb)	Deviation from the Mean (lb)
15	9	6
2	9	7
5	9	4
8	9	1
11	9	2
9	9	0
13	9	4

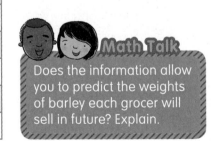

Math Talk

Does the information allow you to predict the weights of barley each grocer will sell in future? Explain.

Mean absolute deviation of the weights of barley Grocer B sold

$$= \frac{6 + 7 + 4 + 1 + 2 + 0 + 4}{7}$$

$$= \frac{24}{7}$$

= 3 lb (to the nearest whole number)

c Compare the means and mean absolute deviations of the weights of barley the two grocers sold. Which grocer's sales of barley showed less variability? Explain.

The mean weight of barley the two grocers sold is the same. The mean absolute deviation of the weights of barley Grocer A sold is less than that of Grocer B. This means that the weights of the barley Grocer A sold are less spread out than those Grocer B sold. So, the weights of the barley Grocer A sold showed less variability.

8 The wait times, in minutes, in two hospitals, A and B, in a month are summarized in the box plots.

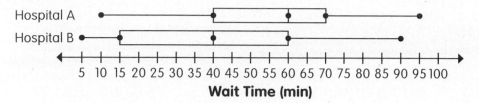

Hospital A
Hospital B

5 10 15 20 25 30 35 40 45 50 55 60 65 70 75 80 85 90 95 100

Wait Time (min)

a Compare the medians of the two hospitals.

b Compare the interquartile ranges of the two hospitals.

c Relate the interquartile ranges to the distributions. Which hospital has a less variability in wait times? Explain.

9 The table shows the mean and mean absolute deviation of the test scores of two classes, A and B.

Test Scores

	Mean	Mean Absolute Deviation
Class A	85	6.8
Class B	78	3.5

Use the means and mean absolute deviations to compare the performances of the two classes.

10 The table shows the time taken, in minutes, by two baristas, P and Q, to each serve ten customers drinks on a certain morning.

Time Taken to Serve Customers Drinks

	Time (min)									
Barista P	8.0	7.5	8.0	9.5	10.0	12.5	12.0	13.5	11.0	14.0
Barista Q	5.5	5.0	10.5	12.0	12.5	13.0	15.5	12.5	16.0	18.5

 a Find the mean time taken, in minutes, by each barista.

 b Calculate the mean absolute deviation of the time taken, in minutes, by each barista.

c Compare the means and mean absolute deviations of the time taken by the two baristas. Which barista showed less variability in the time taken to serve the ten customers? Explain.

Name: _____   Date: _____

Mathematical Habit 2 Use mathematical reasoning

The tables show the statistics for the test scores of two classes, A and B.

Statistics for the Test Scores of Class A

Mean	Median	Mode	Lowest Score	Highest Score	Lower Quartile	Upper Quartile	Mean Absolute Deviation
6.30	6.0	6.0	3.0	10.0	5.0	7.5	1.46

Statistics for the Test Scores of Class B

Mean	Median	Mode	Lowest Score	Highest Score	Lower Quartile	Upper Quartile	Mean Absolute Deviation
7.15	7.5	10.0	2.0	10.0	5.5	9.0	1.95

a Compare the mean, median, and mode of each data set. What can you infer about the distribution of each set of test scores?

b Analyze the statistics in the tables. What can you infer about the variability in the test scores of the two classes?

© 2020 Marshall Cavendish Education Pte Ltd

Problem Solving with Heuristics

1 | Mathematical Habit 1 | **Persevere in solving problems**
The table shows the mean scores of three classes in a history test.

Mean Scores of Three Classes

Class	Mean Score
A	8
B	6
C	9

The mean score of all the students in Classes A and B combined is 6.8 points.
The mean score of all the students in Classes B and C combined is 7 points.
Given that the number of students in Classes A, B, and C are denoted by a, b, and c, respectively, find the ratio $a : b : c$.

2 | Mathematical Habit 1 | **Persevere in solving problems**
Calculate the mean absolute deviation of the data set 1, 2, 5, 7, 8, and 11. Suppose one more data value, $a > 11$, is included in the data set. As a result, the mean absolute deviation increases to 4. What is the value of a?

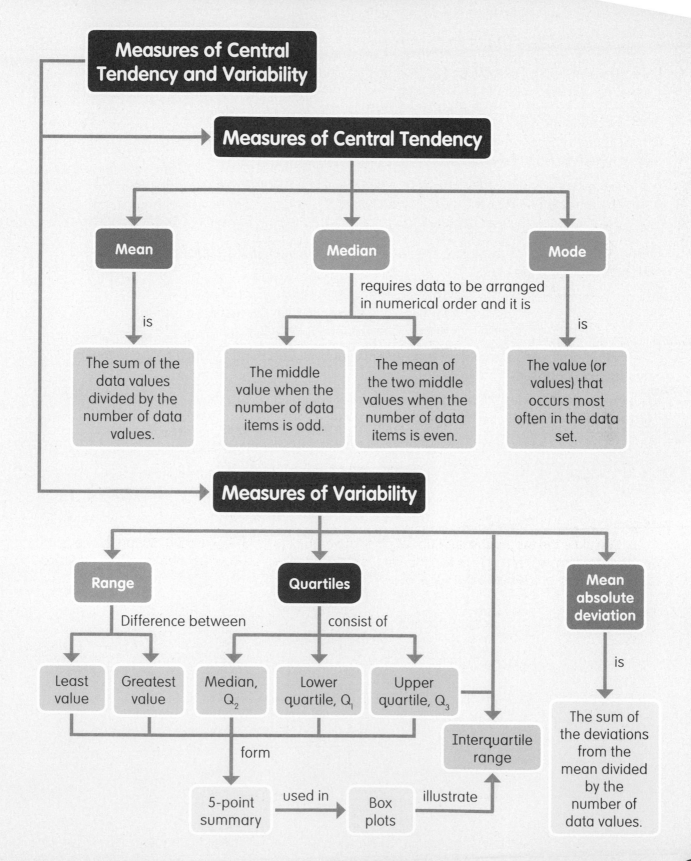

Measures of Central Tendency and Variability

Measures of Central Tendency

Mean

is

The sum of the data values divided by the number of data values.

Median

requires data to be arranged in numerical order and it is

The middle value when the number of data items is odd.

The mean of the two middle values when the number of data items is even.

Mode

is

The value (or values) that occurs most often in the data set.

Measures of Variability

Range

Difference between

Least value

Greatest value

Quartiles

consist of

Median, Q_2

Lower quartile, Q_1

Upper quartile, Q_3

form

5-point summary

used in

Box plots

illustrate

Interquartile range

Mean absolute deviation

is

The sum of the deviations from the mean divided by the number of data values.

KEY CONCEPTS

- The three measures of central tendency are the mean, median, and mode. Each of these three measures is a single number that summarizes all the values in a data set.

- Mean and median are both used to describe the center of a set of numeric data. Mean gives more weight to outliers than median does.

- Mode is the only measure that can be used to describe non-numeric data.

- In a symmetric or nearly symmetric data set, the mean, median, and mode will be close together.

- In a skewed distribution, the median and mode will be close together, but the mean will move towards the outliers.

- Measures of variability are statistics that measure the spread of data.

- Range is a measure of variability. It is the difference between the greatest and the least data values.

- Quartiles are measures of variability that divide data into four equal parts. There are three quartiles: first quartile (or the lower quartile, Q_1), second quartile (or the median, Q_2), and third quartile (or the upper quartile, Q_3).

- The interquartile range is another measure of variability. It is the difference between the third and the first quartiles.

- The mean absolute deviation is also a measure of variability. It is a measure of the average distance of data values from the mean of the data set.

b Calculate the mean absolute deviation of the amount of rainfall, in inches, in each city. Round your answers to the nearest hundredth.

c Compare the means and mean absolute deviations of the amount of rainfall in the two cities. Which city has less variability in the amounts of rainfall? Explain.

Assessment Prep

Answer each question.

13 Which of the following statement(s) is true? Choose all that apply.

(A) Mean absolute deviation describes the absolute value of the mean.

(B) Mean absolute deviation describes the average distance between each data value and the mean.

(C) Mean absolute deviation describes the variability of data values around the median.

(D) Mean absolute deviation describes the variability of data values around the mode.

14 The dot plot shows the number of hours of sleep a group of students had the night before a test.

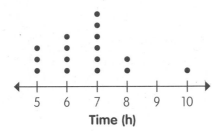

Time (h)

Which of the following statement(s) is true? Choose all that apply.

(A) There are 16 students in the group.

(B) The data is skewed to the left.

(C) The data "10" is an outlier.

(D) The median is 7 hours.

15 Mason took part in five races. His mean race time is 6.4 seconds. His first four race times were 6.9 seconds, 5.8 seconds, 5.9 seconds, and 6.3 seconds. What was his last race time? Write your answer and your work or explanation in the space below.

16 Daniel recorded the temperature at noon, in degrees Fahrenheit, over 12 days.

62   50   54   57   51   53   60   52   50   58   52   54

Find the median, the lower quartile, and the upper quartile of this data set.
Write your answers in the space below.

3 Alexis surveyed 12 customers in the following week. Their shoe sizes are shown below.

10	7	9	8	12	9
9	11	8	10	9	8

a Find the least size, the greatest size, the median, the lower quartile, and the upper quartile.

b Draw a box plot of the shoe sizes.

c Analyzing the box plot, what shoe sizes do you recommend Alexis to order for 50% of her future shoe orders?

d Calculate the mean and mean absolute deviation of the shoe sizes. Round your answers to the nearest whole number.

e Using your answers in **d**, what conclusion can you make about the "typical" shoe sizes of Alexis's customers?

Index

TRY Practice using means and mean absolute deviations to compare two data sets to solve real-world problems

Solve.

1 The table shows the heights, in centimeters, of plants ten students from each group, X and Y, measured in the school garden.

Heights of Plants

	Height (cm)									
Group X	85	94	95	96	97	97	98	100	102	105
Group Y	86	90	92	95	96	96	97	99	100	103

 a Find the mean height, in centimeters, of plants each group measured.

Mean height of plants Group X measured

$$= \frac{\boxed{} + \boxed{} + \boxed{} + \boxed{} + \boxed{} + \boxed{} + \boxed{} + \boxed{} + \boxed{} + \boxed{}}{\boxed{}}$$

$$= \frac{\boxed{}}{\boxed{}}$$

$$= \underline{\hspace{2cm}} \text{ cm}$$

The mean height of plants Group X measured is _____ centimeters.

Mean height of plants Group Y measured

$$= \frac{\boxed{} + \boxed{} + \boxed{} + \boxed{} + \boxed{} + \boxed{} + \boxed{} + \boxed{} + \boxed{} + \boxed{}}{\boxed{}}$$

$$= \frac{\boxed{}}{\boxed{}}$$

$$= \underline{\hspace{2cm}} \text{ cm}$$

The mean height of plants Group Y measured is _____ centimeters.

b Calculate the mean absolute deviation of the heights, in centimeters, of plants each group measured.

Height of Plant Group X Measured (cm)	Mean (cm)	Deviation from the Mean (cm)

Height of Plant Group Y Measured (cm)	Mean (cm)	Deviation from the Mean (cm)

The mean absolute deviation of the heights of plants Group X measured is

_____ centimeters.

The mean absolute deviation of the heights of plants Group Y measured is

_____ centimeters.

c Compare the means and mean absolute deviations of the heights of plants the two groups measured. Which group's measures of the heights of the plants showed greater variability? Explain.

INDEPENDENT PRACTICE

Solve.

1 Eight students took a mathematics quiz. Their scores were 85, 92, 73, 85, 68, 82, 93, and 76. Find the mean, median, and mode.

2 The table shows the results of a survey carried out on 80 families.

Number of Children in 80 Families

Number of Children	0	1	2	3	4	5	6
Number of Families	8	17	21	13	13	6	2

a Find the mean, median, and mode.

b Which measure of central tendency best describes the data set? Explain your answer.

3 The data set shows the weights of ten gerbils in ounces.
3.49, 2.48, 2.57, 2.59, 2.61, 2.57, 2.98, 2.43, 2.45, 2.58

a Find the mean, median, and mode.

b Which one of the weights would you remove from the list if you want the mean to be closer to the median?

4 The dot plot shows the number of hours nine students spent surfing the Internet in a day.
Each dot represents one student.

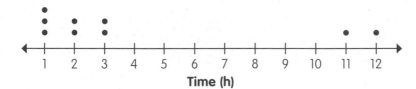

Time (h)

a Find the mean, median, and mode.

b Give a reason why the mean is much greater than the median.

c Which measure of central tendency best describes the data set?

d Relate the measures of center to the shape of the data distribution.

5 The dot plot shows the results of a survey on the number of brothers or sisters each student in a class has. Each dot represents one student.

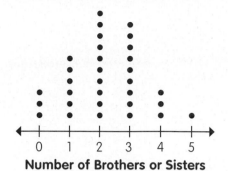

Number of Brothers or Sisters

Briefly describe the data distribution and relate the measure of center to the shape of the dot plot shown.

6 A box contains cards each with a number 1, 2, 3, 4, or 5 on it. In an experiment, 20 students took turns to draw a card from the box. The number written on the card was recorded before it was put back into the box.

Ariana, who was the last person to draw a card, was supposed to complete the dot plot below. However, she lost the record of the experiment's results. All she could recall was the following:

- There were twice as many cards with the number '3' drawn as there were cards with the number '4' drawn.
- There were an equal number of cards with the numbers '1' and '5' drawn.
- 5 cards with the number '2' were drawn.
- 8 students drew cards that show an even number.

a Draw a dot plot to represent the data.

b Briefly describe the data distribution and relate the measure of center to the shape of the dot plot.

7 The table shows the number of students absent from school over a 30-day period.

Number of Students Absent from School

Number of Students	0	1	2	3
Number of Days	8	7	10	5

a What is the mode of this distribution?

b Find the mean and median number of students absent from school over the 30 days.

c It is found that the mean number of students absent from school over a subsequent 20-day period is 1. Find the mean number of students absent from school over the entire 50-day period.

d If 4 students were absent from school instead of 3 on one of the 30 days, what would the mean of the distribution be? Round your answer to the nearest hundredth.

e If on one day of the 30-day period, 2 students were absent from school instead of 1, would the median of the distribution over the 30-day period be affected? If so, what is the new median?

Name: _____ Date: _____

Solve.

1 The data set shows nine students' scores in a science quiz.

9, 6, 6, 5, 9, 10, 1, 4, 10

Find the mean and median score.

2 The mean of a set of four numbers is 3.5. If a fifth number, x, is added to the data set, the mean becomes 4. Find the value of x.

3 The data set shows the number of vehicles at a highway intersection during off-peak hour on 15 working days.

12, 11, 4, 6, 9, 11, 4, 6, 12, 16, 11, 10, 8, 4, 5

a Draw a dot plot to show the data.

b Find the mean, median, and mode of the data set.

4 The data set shows the amount of money 10 adults spent on transport in a week.

$16, $13, $11, $19, $17, $28, $15, $11, $13, $11

a Find the mean and median amount of money spent.

b Which amount of money would you remove from the list if you want the mean to be closer to the median? Explain your answer.

5 Three classes took a geography test last week. The table shows the mean score of the students in each class.

Mean Score of Students in Three Classes

Class	A	B	C
Number of Students	x	25	20
Mean Score	6	8	y

The mean score of the students in Classes A and B combined is 7.25. The mean score of all the students in the three classes is 6.5. Find the values of x and y.

6 The table shows the number of goals scored by a soccer team in 15 games.

Number of Goals Scored by a Soccer Team

Number of Goals	1	2	3	4	5	6	7
Number of Games	5	6	3	0	0	0	1

a Draw a dot plot to show the data.

b Find the mean, median, and mode of the data set.

c Briefly describe the data distribution and relate the measures of center to the shape of the distribution.

7 The dot plot shows the results of a survey to find the number of computers in 30 randomly chosen families. Each dot represents one family.

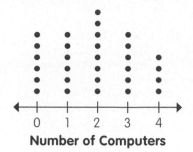

Number of Computers

a What is the modal number of computers?

b What is the mean number of computers? Round your answer to the nearest hundredth.

c What is the median number of computers?

d Briefly describe the data distribution and relate the measures of center to the shape of the dot plot shown.

e A similar survey is carried out on another 15 randomly chosen families and the mean number of computers is found to be 2. If the two data sets are combined, find the mean number of computers in the combined data set. Round your answer to the nearest hundredth.

8 Abigail tossed three number dice 35 times. She found the sum of the values for each throw and displayed the sums in a dot plot.

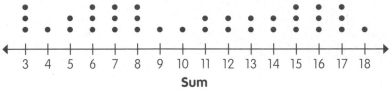

Sum

a Find the range of the data.

b Find the three quartiles of the scores.

c Find the interquartile range.

9 The box plot below summarizes the scores of a basketball team in a game season.

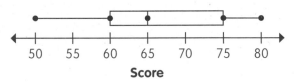

Score

a Find the range of the scores.

b Find the three quartiles of the scores.

c Find the interquartile range.

d Given that the team played in 60 matches, how many matches did they score 60 points and above?

10 The mathematics test scores of a group of students are shown below.

96	85	100	73	78	82	96	84
98	56	73	57	77	97	60	85

a Find the range of the scores.

b Find the three quartiles of the scores.

c Find the interquartile range of the scores.

d Draw a box plot to represent the data.

e Calculate the mean absolute deviation of the scores. Round your answer to the nearest tenth.

11 The ages, in years, of bowlers in two teams, P and Q, are summarized in the box plots.

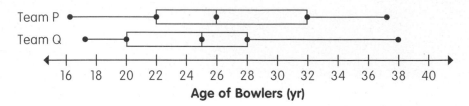

a Compare the median ages of the two teams.

b Compare the interquartile ranges of the two teams.

c Relate the interquartile ranges to the distributions. Which team has a greater variability in ages? Explain.

12 The table shows the amounts of rainfall, in inches, over a certain year in two cities, X and Y.

Amounts of Rainfall (in.) in Two Cities

Month	Jan.	Feb.	Mar.	Apr.	May	Jun.	Jul.	Aug.	Sep.	Oct.	Nov.	Dec.
City X	4.5	4.5	3.3	1.5	0.7	0.2	0.1	0.1	0.2	1.1	3.2	4.6
City Y	3.9	3.3	4.1	3.9	4.5	3.5	4.5	4.1	4.0	3.4	3.8	3.8

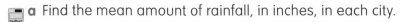

a Find the mean amount of rainfall, in inches, in each city.

Manipulative
   geoboards, *see* Geoboards
   virtual, *see* Virtual manipulative

Maps, 111

Mathematical terms, 4

Mean, **315**, 360–363, 379
   comparing, 338, 368
      two data sets to solve real-world problems,
         367–369
   of data set, 315–316
      comparing, 329–330
      using a dot plot, 317–318
   finding total and missing number from,
      319–320
   height, 369
   length, 317
   real-world problems, 359–361
   scores, 378
   speed, 354
   temperature, 316, 330
   using, to solve problems, 319
   weight, 367

Mean absolute deviation, **352**–354, 379
   comparing, 368
      two data sets to solve real-world problems,
         367–369
   of data set, 352–354, 378
   of heights, 370
   of weights, 368

Measure of variability, **342**, 379

Measures of center
   to shape of data distribution, 363–364

Measures of central tendency, **315**, 363–364, 379
   real-world problems, 359
   skewed or symmetrical distribution, 362–363

Median, **325**, 344, 349–350, 362–363, 379
   comparing, 338, 365–366
   of data set, 325–327
      comparing, 329–330
      using a dot plot, 328–329
   real-world problems, 359–361
   temperature, 330

Missing number, in equation, 54

Mode, **335**, 362–363, 379
   comparing, 338
   of data set, 335–336
   real-world problems, 359–361
   summarize categorical data set using, 337

Mosaic, 155

Multiplication, 10
   solving algebraic equations using, 62–63
   writing algebraic expressions by, 9–10

Nearest, 313

Negative numbers on number line, 113

Net, **217**
   identify
      of cube, 217–218
      of prism, 221
      of pyramid, 223–224
      of rectangular prism, 219–220, 222
      of triangular prism, 219–220, 222
   of solids, 224

Number lines, 115, 274
   horizontal, *see* Horizontal number lines
   negative numbers on, 113
   pictorial representations, 84, 87–88, 99, 113, 313

Numbers
   absolute value of, 113, 313
   common factors of, 4
   greatest common factor of, 4
   whole, *see* Whole numbers

Number wheel, 335

Numerical data
   representation
      dot plot to, 273–275
      histograms to, 281–282

Odd number of values, 326

One variable, 100

Ordered pair, 116

Photo Credits

1m: © Michal Bednarek/Dreamstime.com, 1m: © Marina Lohrbach/123rf.com, 1b: © Diana Taliun/123rf.com, 1b: © Alisonh29/Dreamstime.com, 52t: Teerawut Masawat/123rf.com, 52br: Roman Kyryliuk/123rf.com, 52lb: Roman Kyryliuk/123rf.com, 53: © Sunanta Boonkamonsawat/123rf.com, 98m: Atikan Pornchaiprasit/123rf.com, 98m: Thampapon Otavorn/123rf.com, 111: pics721/shutterstock.com, 143: fwstudio/freepik.com, 154t: mingazitdinov/123rf.com, 154m: Sanchai Khudpin/123rf.com, 155: sumetho/123rf.com, 155ml: Eugene Sergeev/123rf.com, 155r: iSTock/1 credit, 155l: agafapaperiapunta/iStock, 155mr: dmanjoe/iStock, 201: fwstudio/freepik.com, 213mr: © Brostock/Dreamstime.com, 213ml: ©Snowingg/Dreamstime.com, 251: fwstudio/freepik.com, 265f: © stillraining/123rf.com, 265b: © Black_J B/123rf.com, 295: fwstudio/freepik.com, 310t: Cathy Yeulet/123rf.com, 310b: Sergey Novikov/123rf.com, 311: © TEA/ 123rf.com, 377: fwstudio/freepik.com, 391bl: serezniy/123rf.com

NOTES

NOTES

NOTES

NOTES

NOTES